THE
AUTOMATIC CUSTOMER

THE
AUTOMATIC
CUSTOMER

Creating a Subscription Business
in Any Industry

John Warrillow

Portfolio / Penguin

PORTFOLIO / PENGUIN
Published by the Penguin Group
Penguin Group (USA) LLC
375 Hudson Street
New York, New York 10014

USA | Canada | UK | Ireland | Australia | New Zealand | India | South Africa | China
penguin.com
A Penguin Random House Company

First published by Portfolio / Penguin, a member of Penguin Group (USA) LLC, 2015

Illustration credits
Pages 142, 143, 173: Shockwave Innovations, www.shockwaveinnovations.com
186: J. D. Power 2014 U.S. Retail Banking Satisfaction Study
190: Dmitry Buterin

LIBRARY OF CONGRESS CATALOGING-IN-PUBLICATION DATA

Warrillow, John, 1971-
The automatic customer : creating a subscription business in any industry / John Warrillow.
pages cm
Includes bibliographical references and index.
ISBN 978-1-59184-746-5
1. Entrepreneurship.　2. Business planning.　3. Strategic planning.　I. Title.
HB615.W37 2015
658.8'7—dc23　2014038637

Printed in the United States of America
1　3　5　7　9　10　8　6　4　2

Set in Generis Serif Com
Designed by Alissa Rose Theodor

CONTENTS

Introduction

We had been running together for five months when Sacha announced he was leaving on a business trip to China. The timing could not have been worse; the marathon was just six weeks away, and we had come to rely on each other to stay motivated through the hardest part of our training schedule.

Now, at the height of our work, he was leaving for two weeks.

Since Sacha and I wouldn't be able to run together, we decided to egg each other on digitally. We agreed to text each other the results from our training run each day as a way to stay motivated. Sacha asked if, instead of texting, we could use a messaging service called WhatsApp.

I was used to texting using the standard service on my iPhone, so I wasn't in a hurry to learn a new platform. I asked him why we couldn't just text the normal way.

Sacha replied that the phone company charges a relative fortune to text from China, and WhatsApp, instead of using the mobile networks, mobile carrier fees. In fact, the only fee to use WhatsApp is a $1 per year subscription it charges after the first year.

We used WhatsApp to communicate while Sacha was in China, and eventually finished the marathon together, thanks in part to our WhatsApp-supported training regimen. It turns out that, in using WhatsApp, we were not alone. By early 2014, WhatsApp had acquired 450 million users and was adding a million users per day when Facebook announced it had acquired the company for $19 billion—the largest acquisition of an Internet start-up in history.

Most of the other Internet-based messaging services at the time used an advertising model to monetize their users. They offered a free platform but bombarded users with cheesy ads in return. WhatsApp founders Jan Koum and Brian Acton wanted to offer a cleaner, more private messaging experience. Instead of selling advertising, they opted for the subscription business model.

A dollar a year as a subscription fee may not sound like much, but when you have 450 million users and are picking up a million users a day, $1 a year starts to add up. What's more, because WhatsApp doesn't try to be anything other than a subscription-based messaging platform, it doesn't need a lot of employees. In fact, at the time of its acquisition, it had just 55 people taking care of its 450 million subscribers.

WhatsApp won the $19 billion lottery not because its technology was better, or its people were any more caring, or its advertising was funnier. WhatsApp won, in large part, because it made its customers automatic. It chose the right business model for success by asking users to subscribe to its service.

This book will show you how to apply the subscription business model to your own business. When people think of subscriptions, they often think of cloud-based software, gaming, or media companies. While readers from those industries will benefit from this book, you can also apply the subscription business model to your company—no matter what your size or industry. WhatsApp is only one example of how powerful automatic customers can be for the growth of your business.

I Screwed Up

The last time I wrote a book, I screwed up.

Called *Built to Sell: Creating a Business That Can Thrive Without You,* the book was designed to illustrate how to transform a successful business into a sellable one. In it, I touched briefly on the importance of having customers who repurchase from you on a regular schedule, but in hindsight, I should have dedicated at least half the book to recurring revenue.

In the years since *Built to Sell* was published, I've come to see how important recurring revenue is in building a valuable, sellable company. These days I run a subscription business called The Sellability Score (SellabilityScore.com) that helps owners build valuable companies by examining the eight key drivers of sellability. Owners who achieve a Sellability Score of 80 or more out of a possible 100 garner offers that are 71% higher than the average.

The biggest factor in driving up your Sellability Score is the degree to which your company can run without you, the owner. That's a head scratcher for a lot of owners who are the best salesperson in their business. The secret is to build recurring revenue that brings in sales without having to resell the customer each month.

To appreciate the impact of recurring revenue on your company's value, you have to understand what buyers are buying when they acquire a business. Most owners want buyers to value their past achievements, such as last year's profits or an industry award they're proud of. In fact, it has been my experience that financial buyers are really buying only one thing when they purchase a company: a *future* stream of profits.

In the home security business, for example, companies have two forms of revenue. They receive *installation revenue* when they come to your home or office to install the keypad and wire things up, and they receive *monitoring revenue* in the form of the monthly payment for keeping an eye on things.

At SellabilityScore.com, we know from our analysis that when an acquirer buys a security business, it pays 75 cents for "one-shot" installation revenue and $2 for every dollar of monitoring revenue. Said another way, a security company with 100% monitoring revenue (the subscription aspect of such a business) is almost three times more valuable than a security business of the same size that has 100% installation revenue.

The same trend plays out across most industries. Accounting firms are valued based on their recurring fees. Financial planning practices trade based on how likely clients are to stay with the firm after the owner retires. IBM's stock moves up and down based on its recurring revenue from service contracts.

So recurring revenue makes your business a lot more valuable, and it also makes your company less stressful to run.

The Tyranny of Selling & Doing

In 1997, I started Warrillow & Co., a research company. We started out as a typical "sell/do" services business; our job was to cultivate relationships with people, listen to their problems, and try to come up with a solution. Each project was different, and we spent the majority of our time developing custom proposals, many of which were never accepted.

The company was profitable on paper but debilitatingly stressful to run. I hated the first day of each month because that was when all the dials turned back to zero and we had to scramble to find enough business to cover our overhead.

I remember distinctly the first time our fixed expenses crested $100,000 per month. I thought to myself, "If we don't sell anything this month, we still have $100,000 in expenses to cover!"

The stress of having to re-create the business from scratch each month led me in search of a better model. I started to study other research companies, like Gartner and Forrester Research, that had successfully "productized" a service and, as a result, began experimenting with automating parts of our business.

Instead of doing "one-shot" research, we decided to offer the identical packages of information to a subscriber base of customers. Instead of doing custom proposals, we created a brochure about our offering and a standard proposal. Instead of getting paid 60 days after the project was complete, we charged up front for an annual subscription to our research.

The business became much less stressful to run. We went into each new month with revenue on the books, and we were no longer beholden to any one customer. In fact, we starting winning the world's largest companies as subscribers, including American Express, Apple, AT&T, Bank of America, Dell, FedEx, Google, HP, IBM, MasterCard, Microsoft, Sprint, Visa, and Wells Fargo. Charging for our subscription up front also meant that after a while we had more cash than we knew what to do with. To top it off, we were growing at a rate of 25% a year and were quickly replacing the revenue from the one-shot projects we had left behind. Warrillow & Co. was acquired by a public company in 2008.

You may be thinking, *That's nice, but it would never work in* my *industry or in* my *company.* Maybe—especially if you cling to the standard industry practices of your category. But as you'll see, virtually every business—from a start-up to a Fortune 500 company, from a home contractor to a manufacturer—can create at least some recurring revenue if it is willing to jettison the old way of doing things to pioneer a new business model.

And companies that don't just might face competition from those that do. Increasingly, some of the smallest businesses in the world are facing crippling competition from the largest. The subscription economy has pitted small companies against big ones and suppliers against resellers, and has even made partners into enemies. The battle lines are being drawn, and I hope *The Automatic Customer* will be your secret weapon for winning in the subscription economy.

If you are someone who has a business that you would like to make a little more predictable, a little less stressful, and a whole lot more valuable, this book is for you. Whether you want to transform your entire business model or just pick up an extra 5% of automatic revenue, I hope you'll see yourself in the following pages.

What You'll Find Inside

The book is organized into three sections. Part One outlines the surprising truth about who is winning in the subscription economy, why companies like Apple and Amazon are transforming themselves into subscription businesses, and why virtually every venture-backed start-up has a recurring revenue model.

We'll also look at eight ways your business will be more valuable and less stressful after you adopt the subscription model. You'll learn how the subscription business model dramatically increases the average value of each of your customers, and how to smooth out demand in your company so that it matches your ability to fulfill it. We'll discuss why automatic customers buy more than one-shot customers and why subscription revenue is stickier than a one-time purchase.

Part Two is divided into minichapters on the nine subscription business models. As you'll see, you have a variety of choices when it comes to building a recurring revenue stream for your business. Whether you want to transform your entire business or just pick up a few thousand dollars of passive income, you'll get a ton of new ideas for applying the subscription model to your company.

The third and final section of *The Automatic Customer* gives you the blueprint for building your subscription business. We'll discuss a handful of key statistics that will define the viability of your subscription and highlight one ratio you must achieve in order to scale up. We'll look at the psychology of selling your subscription and how to overcome something I call "subscription fatigue." Then we'll turn to financing the growth of your subscription business and explore whether you want to raise venture-capital funding, as WhatsApp and Dollar Shave Club did, or self-fund your growth, like FreshBooks and Mosquito Squad. Part Three ends with a discussion on scaling your subscription business.

Let's get started.

PART ONE

Subscribers Are Better than Customers

Why are Amazon, Apple, and many of the most promising Silicon Valley start-ups leveraging a subscription business model? In Part One we'll look at how automatic customers make your company more valuable . . . and a whole lot more enjoyable to run.

CHAPTER 1

Who Wins in the Subscription Economy?

Amazon has come a long way since its days of just hawking cheap books online. Of course, you can still buy books on the site, but today's Amazon will sell you everything from diapers to laundry detergent. Increasingly, it is digging deeper into our pockets through the subscription service called Amazon Prime.

Amazon Prime subscribers pay Amazon $99 a year in return for goodies like free streaming of thousands of movies and TV shows and free two-day shipping on most Amazon purchases. According to a 2013 report released by Consumer Intelligence Research Partners, there are now approximately 16 million subscribers to Amazon Prime. As I write this, the folks at Morningstar estimate, since Amazon does not release the data publicly, that membership in Amazon Prime could swell to 25 million by 2017.

If you were to carve out Amazon Prime as a stand-alone business, it would already be a billion-dollar subscription company, but that severely underestimates the value of Prime to Amazon. Like many subscription models, Amazon Prime is a Trojan horse that is expanding the list of products consumers are willing to buy from Amazon and giving the eggheads in Seattle a mountain of customer data to sift through.

"It was never about the $79," said Vijay Ravindran, who worked on the team that launched Prime at its original price of $79 per year. "It was really about changing people's mentality so they wouldn't shop anywhere else."[1]

According to Morningstar, the average Prime member now spends $1,224 on Amazon purchases each year, compared with $505 for non-Prime customers.[2] We cannot say Prime members spend that much more just *because* they are members, since presumably a lot of Amazon's best customers would have been attracted to the free shipping offer. However, this data seems to suggest that once someone becomes a Prime subscriber, they become even more loyal to Amazon. Further, Morningstar figures that after factoring in costs incurred for shipping and streaming content, the average Prime member yields Amazon $78 more per year in *profits* than the typical customer.

Given the positive impact Prime seems to have on customers' buying behavior, some analysts have argued that Amazon should drop the fee for subscribing to Prime in order to grow the program even faster. But that thinking misses a key element of Amazon's strategy. When you pay $99 per year to become a member, you want to "get your money's worth." Suddenly you start checking Amazon's pricing on all sorts of products, from paper towels to sneakers, with hopes of "making back" what you invested in the membership. Given Amazon's aggressive pricing and seemingly endless product selection, you can almost always find what you're looking for at a price that's lower than what you could find elsewhere. When you factor in free shipping, it becomes an easy decision to buy from Amazon.

Robbie Schwietzer, vice president of Amazon Prime from 2008 to 2013, summarized: "In all my years here, I don't remember anything that has been as successful at getting customers to shop in new product lines."[3]

Through Prime, Amazon is competing head-to-head with the likes of Walmart and Target. Why should you care if three heavyweights are pounding it out for market supremacy? Because as customers buy a broader and broader collection of items from Amazon, Prime is cannibalizing the business of smaller companies too.

The other day I bought a pair of New Balance running shoes from Amazon. I've never thought to use Amazon for buying sneakers, but since I am now a Prime member, and therefore get free shipping on shoes, I chose Amazon instead of walking down the street to my local Running Room store.

The Running Room is a small company compared to Amazon, with 100 or so locations scattered around North America. Most people would not consider Amazon a direct competitor. Yet the Running Room is now losing my shoe-buying business because of a little $99-per-year Prime subscription I bought.

Everything by Subscription

Amazon, having learned a lot about the subscription business through Prime, is now applying the subscription model to other areas of its business. AmazonFresh is a grocery delivery business Amazon has been experimenting with in its hometown of Seattle since 2007. Amazon Fresh didn't start out as a subscription business; instead, it was open to anyone willing to pay the delivery fee of $8 to $10 to have milk, veggies, and meat brought to their door in a one- to three-hour delivery window.

AmazonFresh stayed stuck in beta in one city for six years as the company tried to work out a profitable business model. The business proved challenging, which Amazon founder Jeff Bezos seemed to acknowledge in response to a question about AmazonFresh at Amazon's 2013 annual shareholders meeting: "They have made progress on the economics over the last year," said Bezos.[4] "They've been doing a lot of experiments and trying to get the right mixture of customer experience and economics. I'm optimistic that the team is making good progress."[5]

In spring 2013, AmazonFresh added Los Angeles as the second city for the program. But in L.A., the Amazon Fresh offer had one stark difference: L.A.-based customers were asked to *subscribe* to Prime Fresh for $299 a year, which gave them free grocery delivery on orders over $35.

As with Amazon Prime, the act of subscribing spurs Prime Fresh members to buy more frequently and from a broader array of grocery categories. If I'm ordering milk anyway, a customer might reason, why not top up the order north of $35 with a case of Coke and a refill on the laundry detergent I'm about to run out of? As with Prime, the very act of sinking money into a subscription triggers the desire for the consumer to want to "get his money's worth," which in turn creates the kind of customer behavior Amazon wants to see. And Amazon isn't stopping at groceries: Subscribe & Save is yet another subscription service from Amazon; you subscribe to receive regular shipments of things you frequently run out of, like dish soap and paper towels. If you sign up for five or more subscriptions that share the same delivery date, you receive 15% off the entire order.

As more consumers consolidate their buying on Amazon's subscriptions, the competition is reacting. In the fall of 2013, Minneapolis-based Target launched Target Subscriptions, a program similar to Subscribe & Save. Not surprisingly, its first focus was on baby products like diapers and wipes—a category Amazon placed a big bet on when it paid $545 million to acquire Quidsi, the creators of Diapers.com, which itself offers a subscription for diapers that enjoyed 30% month-over-month growth in 2013.[6]

Amazon is known for its wins in selling to consumers—but subscriptions can work for B2B as well as B2C. One of Amazon's latest ventures is a subscription that offers to help other companies grow *their* subscription businesses. Amazon Web Services (AWS) offers companies access to servers, software, and technology support on a subscription basis. Many of the world's largest subscription companies, including Adobe, Citrix, Netflix, and Sage, use AWS, along with many of the highest-profile start-ups, like Airbnb, Pinterest, Dropbox, and Spotify.

Amazon is pioneering the subscription model in virtually every area of its business, but the subscription model is nothing new. In fact, it's been around for quite a while.

A (Very) Short History of the Subscription Model

The history of the subscription business model dates back to the 1500s, when European map publishers would invite their customers to subscribe to future editions of their maps, which were evolving as new lands were discovered, conquered, and claimed. The geopolitical landscape was evolving, and map publishers would obtain commitments from members of the noble and academic classes to subscribe to future volumes of their maps, giving the publishers the capital they needed to plot the world's discoveries on paper.

This model was then applied to early newspapers and magazines, dating back to the periodicals of 17th-century Europe.[7] Eventually the subscription model became the standard business approach for information publishing. Readers were asked to subscribe to general interest publications, and their subscription fees, combined with advertising revenue, provided the money needed to fund the editorial product and the cost of mailing the publication to each reader. This trend continued well into the 20th century, as it was also a reliable way to get rich. Publishers like William Randolph Hearst and, more recently, Rupert Murdoch have made their initial fortunes from publishing subscription-based newspapers.

However, the economics of information publishing deteriorated with the rise of the Internet, which eliminated distribution costs and commoditized content to such an extent that consumers began to expect it to be free. Not only did consumers expect content for free; the kind of content they were interested in also became more esoteric. As former *Wired* magazine editor Chris Anderson revealed in his best seller *The Long Tail,* now that the entire world's content is only a Google search away, we are no longer satisfied with the broad general interest information provided by mainstream publishers; our appetite for content has become more specialized. If you love the sport of curling, you can consume as much curling information as you want for free online without ever picking up a newspaper, which might run a curling story a couple of times per winter at best.

Thus the traditional publishing model was under attack from two sides: information was becoming commoditized, and our appetite for it was becoming more specialized. Magazines and newspapers started slashing editorial budgets, with fewer and fewer subscribers underwriting the costs of creating content and mailing it out.

Content got so bad that people began realizing that good content was actually worth paying for—and subscriptions took on a new life in the information industry. First, the *Wall Street Journal* courageously put its best content behind a paywall in 1997 and gained 200,000 paying customers within 18 months.[8] In 2007, the *Financial Times* introduced a "metered model" paywall. Readers received 10 articles for free before being asked to sign up, then were awarded 30 more articles. After they used up their 30 articles, they were asked to pay an annual subscription of up to $325. By 2011, the *Wall Street Journal* eclipsed 1 million paying online subscribers, and the *New York Times*—arguably the most influential media outlet in the world—erected a metered paywall, which by 2013 had 700,000 subscribers for the online product.[9]

Around the same time that the *Wall Street Journal* put up its paywall, Silicon Valley fell in love with the subscription business model. In the late 1990s, application service providers such as Onvia offered access to computer applications on a subscription basis rather than requiring users to load up their software from a CD. While some of the early players were weeded out during the "tech wreck" of 2001, the business model lived on in software as a service (SaaS) businesses and in "cloud-based" companies such as Salesforce.com and Constant Contact.

The Subscription Model Renaissance

Basically, while the subscription business model has been around for centuries, over the last two decades it has been revitalized by technology and media companies. Most recently, a confluence of four factors has ushered in a subscription model renaissance across all industries.

The Access Generation

In 2013, the home ownership rate in the United States dropped to an 18-year low.[10] One reason lay in the behavior of the millennial generation. Unlike their baby-boomer parents, for whom the American Dream meant a house in the suburbs, today's twenty- and thirty-somethings are delaying marriage, kids, and a house in the suburbs in favor of renting in the city.

Given a mountain of student debt and a difficult job market, many young people couldn't afford to buy a house even if they wanted one. But for many in the millennial generation, assets are viewed as a yoke restricting their mobility.

Call them the Access Generation: a growing cohort of mobile, technically savvy young people who value access over assets. They prefer to stay nimble and rent a home rather than own one; listen to a song on Spotify rather than buy it from iTunes; or subscribe to Oysterbooks .com or Scribd rather than buy from a Barnes & Noble store.

The Access Generation is behind the explosion of the new "sharing" economy. Sharing stuff has been around since stuff itself, but technology allows sharing to scale: websites like Airbnb match buyer and seller; your GPS-enabled iPhone allows you to find the closest Zipcar; Facebook and LinkedIn enable you to vet anyone you're thinking of doing business with; and sites like PayPal allow you to safely pay for what you're renting.

Light-Switch Reliability

When you walk into a room and turn on the light, you don't hold your breath hoping the room will illuminate. You just expect the lights to come on because electricity has become so dependable. The Internet is becoming almost as pervasive and reliable. Two decades ago you would have to search for a place to plug in your laptop for a dial-up connection. Today we just expect Wi-Fi wherever we go, from a hotel to a friend's basement to a plane 30,000 feet in the air.

The more reliable Internet access has become, the more we are willing to entrust to the Internet. Nowadays, we do everything from our banking to our socializing online.

When you can rely on a subscription service like Salesforce.com to house all of your company's private customer data, or your bank's website to pay your electricity bill, buying a $19-per-month subscription to dog treats from BarkBox.com doesn't seem that risky. Matt Meeker, BarkBox's founder, elaborates: "BarkBox wouldn't have made much sense back when there wasn't much trust in online commerce and the Internet was slower."[11] Companies like BarkBox are possible today because we have become more trusting of online commerce. There was a time when we would hand over our credit card information only to the most "blue chip" of companies. Today, many of us give over our digits to even fledgling start-ups.

Delicious Data

Do you remember the old distribution channel structure they taught in high school? If you close your eyes, you can probably see the flow-chart: manufacturers sell to distributors; distributors sell to retailers, who sell to the end customer.

In that model, you needed to rely on "the channel" for information on customer preferences. If you wanted to know if consumers wanted their widgets in green or red, you asked the channel.

Today, businesses are closer to their end users than ever before. Many consumers buy directly through an online channel, and those who don't often interact with the producer directly for post-sale service or support. All those customer interactions are being fed into mathematical models, which are run by computers that are now capable of storing and processing billions of data points in seconds. That's why, after you rate *The West Wing* with five stars, Netflix's data can predict you'll like *House of Cards.*

Data has become an asset, and nobody has more customer information than a subscription business. Traditional companies are launching entire subscription offerings just for the data they provide.

Between 2012 and 2013, Walmart's innovation incubator @Wal martLabs ran the subscription business Goodies Co. For a flat fee of $7 a month, Goodies delivered a box of sample-size treats to your doorstep. If you liked the product, you could purchase the full-size version on the Goodies Co. website.

Walmart gained insight on subscribers not only through their purchases but also via a product-rating system on the Goodies website that let subscribers review the items they had sampled. Goodies then rewarded reviewers for their contributions with loyalty points they could earn through rating, writing a review, or uploading a photo. If subscribers earned enough points, they could trade them in to get their next month's box free.

Walmart didn't launch Goodies Co. for the purpose of making a measly $7 a month. The world's largest retailer wanted to know which snacks resonated enough to make you want to buy the full-size version. Goodies Co. subscribers helped Walmart understand how the consumer's appetite for snacks had evolved, which helped it buy the right items to sell in its stores.

The Long Tail

As Chris Anderson argued in *The Long Tail*, the Internet has lowered the cost of distribution for many products and services, and our appetites have broadened as a result.

As Anderson recounts, there was a time when you bought books in a bookstore. The bookstore paid rent and therefore had to stock only the best-selling books to ensure that sales revenue per square foot was high enough to cover its rent and staff. If you liked John Grisham or Jim Collins, you were fine, but if your reading tastes were a touch more exotic, you were screwed.

Today, the cost of merchandising products digitally is close to zero, so companies no longer need to carry just "hits." As a result, we're expressing our individuality. If you have a thing for salsa dancing, you can listen to hundreds of hours of cha-cha-cha with your subscription to Spotify. If all we cared to listen to was Coldplay and Beyoncé, there would be no need for a Spotify subscription—we'd just buy their latest albums. If you like British crime drama, there's no need to wait for the movie of the week on cable; you can now watch Inspector Morse any time of the day or night with your streaming subscription to Netflix. If you love chocolate, you can buy a Dairy Milk bar at your local Walgreens, but increasingly chocolate lovers are subscribing to New York–based Standard Cocoa for $25 per month and receiving a hand-picked selection of chocolate from around the world each month.

Customers want to express their individuality, and increasingly they are using subscriptions to do that.

Competing in the New Subscription Economy

These four factors—the access generation, light-switch reliability, delicious data, and the long tail—have led some of the world's most successful companies and promising start-ups to shift their business models to a focus on subscriptions. Take Apple, for example. Apple used to be thought of as a product for consumers, not a product for businesses. Businesses shunned Apple in favor of industry standard Microsoft— but that was before Apple, now the world's most successful technology company, found a new way to get customers for its products.

This new project is called Joint Venture. Launched in 2011, it was inspired in part by Apple's One to One subscription department, where a million consumers pay $99 a year for special access to Apple's troubleshooters. With Joint Venture, Apple will help a business get up and running using Mac products, in return for a $499-per-year subscription. Apple will set up your company's computers and migrate your old data, in addition to training your employees in using their new Macs. Joint Venture subscribers also get special access to Apple's Genius Bar and can get a free loaner computer if their Mac needs to be serviced.

Why should you care how Apple makes another hundred million dollars? First, Apple is a smart company, and if a new business model works for Apple, it is worth understanding to see if there are lessons that apply to your business. Second, the hundred million dollars Apple gets from One to One—and also the billions that other Fortune 500 companies now glean from similar subscription models—may be coming out of *your* pocket.

Apple's One to One offering cannibalizes part of the value proposition of its Apple Reseller network. These small independent businesses survive by selling and servicing Apple hardware and taking a tiny commission. Since some people would rather get their questions answered directly from the company instead of a middleman, One to One is likely to lessen demand for these businesses.

Like Apple and Amazon, cable TV giant Time Warner Cable recently launched a subscription service, called SignatureHome, that provides special access to its service staff. For $199 per month, subscribers receive a television package and Internet access, a specially trained technician to customize all their devices, and a team of "personal solutions advisers" who are available anytime by online chat and phone. Subscribers also get special access to scheduled service calls at preferred times. If Time Warner Cable has to send a technician to a SignatureHome subscriber's house, he or she will wear specially designed booties to keep the customer's floors tidy—a small touch designed to make SignatureHome subscribers feel valued.

Similarly, Microsoft has also made plays in the area of subscription services with Microsoft Office, the most successful and pervasive software program in history. The folks in Redmond don't want you *buying* Office at Staples anymore; today, they want to sell you a subscription to Office 365. Microsoft's aggressive push into cloud computing has been accelerated by Google Apps, another office productivity suite that is available to businesses exclusively through subscription.

Big companies like Apple, Time Warner Cable, Amazon, Target, Microsoft, and Google are not necessarily walking away from their traditional business models entirely. In many cases, they are *adding* a subscription business to build recurring revenue, expand their relationships with existing customers, and understand what customers want. Research firm Gartner estimates that "by 2015, 35% of Global 2000 companies with non-media digital products will generate incremental revenue of 5% to 10% through subscription-based services and revenue models."[12]

Whether you like it or not, you are now competing in the new subscription economy, and it's up to you to decide if you're playing defense or offense. Defensive players will decide how to minimize the impact of subscription offerings from giant companies like Amazon and Apple. Ultimately they will shrink and live on the economy's table scraps.

Or, like Alex Hyssen, you can play offense and launch a subscription offering of your own.

What the Cool Kids Are Doing

Køge is a promising Toronto-based start-up cofounded by Alex Hyssen, the son of Dr. James Hyssen, one of the cofounders of Herbal Magic

Weight Loss & Nutrition Centers, which offer weight-loss programs and supplements through 280 bricks-and-mortar stores across Canada.

Køge is also a vitamin retailer, but instead of following in his dad's footsteps, Hyssen has opted to use the subscription business model. For $49.99 per month, you can subscribe to a monthly regimen of daily essential vitamins delivered to your doorstep. Once you sign up and pick a vitamin bundle based on your health objectives, the annoying, repetitive task of buying vitamins is checked off your to-do list for good.

Many of the world's most promising start-ups are now leveraging the subscription business model to win new customers, romance their existing fans, and improve cash flow. According to a 2013 study by the Economist Intelligence Unit, over half of surveyed companies are changing the way they deliver products and service. Four in five companies surveyed believe their customers are switching to new consumption models like sharing or subscribing. Of the companies changing the way they price and deliver goods, 40% are adopting the subscription business model.

But the market for any given commodity is a zero-sum game. For every customer who decides to subscribe to a vitamin regimen from Køge, one less person buys vitamins from the local health food store. For every customer who subscribes to receive their Puppy Chow from Amazon's Subscribe & Save, one less dog lover visits her local pet supplies store.

So what's it going to be? Are you willing to watch your business be cannibalized by someone else's subscription business? Or are you ready to win some automatic customers of your own?

CHAPTER 2

Why You Need Automatic Customers

Massive companies like Amazon, Apple, and Microsoft are adopting the subscription model to tighten their already firm grip on our wallets.

So what? Why should you care? Your company doesn't have a hundred billion dollars in revenue, nor are you some start-up backed by venture capital.

Did you pick up the wrong book? No.

I think Mike McDerment, CEO and cofounder of the subscription business FreshBooks.com, said it best when we spoke about the subscription business model back in 2014: "It's the best damn business model in the world . . . it's got great predictability for planning, which helps you as an entrepreneur sleep at night."

In this chapter, I'll make the case for why you need to consider a subscription model in your company *no matter the size of your business or the industry you're in.* Here are the eight reasons subscribers are better than customers.

1. They Increase the Value of Your Largest Asset

If you're like most business owners, your largest asset is not your house or a portfolio of stocks. Your wealth is tied up in your business and how it is valued by potential buyers. Let's take a closer look at how your company is valued *without* a subscription offering.

In my experience, the most common methodology used to value a small to mid-size business is called discounted cash flow. This methodology forecasts your future stream of profits and then "discounts" it back to what your future profit is worth to an investor in today's dollars given the time value of money. This investment theory may sound like MBA talk, but discounted cash flow valuation is something you have likely applied in your own personal life without knowing it. For example, what would you pay today for an investment that you hope will be worth $100 one year from now? You would likely "discount" the $100 by your expectation for a return on investment. If you expect to earn a 7% return on your money each year, you'd pay $93.46 ($100 divided by 1.07) today for an investment you expect to be worth $100 in 12 months.

Using the discounted cash flow valuation methodology, the more profit the acquirer expects your company to make in the future—and the more reliable your estimates—the more your company is worth.

Therefore, to improve the value of a traditional business, the two most important levers you have are (1) how much profit you expect to make in the future and (2) the reliability of those estimates.

At SellabilityScore.com, we see the effect of this valuation methodology every day. Since 2012, we have been tracking the offers received by business owners who complete our questionnaire.

During that time, the average business with at least $3 million in revenue has been offered 4.6 times its pretax profit.

Therefore, a traditional business churning out 10% of pretax profit on $5 million in revenue may reasonably expect to be worth around $2,300,000 ($5,000,000 x 10% x 4.6).

Now let's compare the traditional company with the value of a subscription business. When an acquirer looks at a healthy subscription company, she sees an annuity stream of revenue throwing off years of profit into the future. This predictable stream of future profits means she is willing to pay a significant premium over what she would give for a traditional company. How much of a premium depends on the industry. Some of the biggest premiums today go to companies in the software industry.

To understand what is going on in the valuation of subscription-based software companies, I spoke with Dmitry Buterin. Buterin runs a subscription software company called Wild Apricot. He also formed one of the world's first mastermind groups of small and mid-size subscription company founders. Each month, the group meets to discuss strategies for running a subscription business.

Members of the group were constantly raising money or being courted by investors, so the topic of valuation came up a lot in their conversations. Buterin found the consensus valuation range being offered to his members' companies to be between 24 and 60 times monthly recurring revenue (MRR), which is equivalent to two to five times annual recurring revenue (ARR).

I wanted to validate Buterin's numbers, so I met with another guru from the world of subscription-based software companies named Zane Tarence. Tarence is a partner with Birmingham, Alabama–based

Founders Investment Banking; the company specializes in selling software companies that use the subscription business model. Tarence estimates the valuation ranges he sees as belonging in one of three buckets:

24–48 x MRR (2–4 times ARR)

These are typically very small software companies with less than $5 million in recurring annual revenue. Companies in this first bucket are usually growing modestly, with subscription cancellation rates (i.e., "churn") in the area of 2–4% per month.

48–72 x MRR (4–6 times ARR)

These are larger software companies with recurring revenue of at least $5 million annually, which they are growing at the rate of 25–50% per year. Their net churn is typically below 1.5% per month.

72–96 x MRR (6–8 times ARR)

These are the rare, fast-growth software companies that are growing more than 50% per year, with at least $5 million in annual revenue and net churn below 1% per month. These companies usually offer a solution (typically an industry-specific one) that their customers need to use to get their jobs done.

Even mature, slower-growth subscription businesses sell for a significant premium. The company behind Ancestry.com was started back in 1983 and came of age as a dot-com in the late 1990s. By the end of 2012, Ancestry.com had 2 million subscribers and annual revenue across all of its sites of $487 million, up about 25% from the previous year.[1] On December 28, 2012, before the recent run-up in the valuation of cloud-based companies, Ancestry.com was acquired for $1.6 billion, or 39 times its MRR of approximately $40.5 million.

The software business is an extreme example of the benefits of subscription revenue, but no matter what industry you're in, your company will likely command a premium if it enjoys recurring revenue.

Security businesses that monitor alarm systems and charge a recurring monthly monitoring fee to do so are worth around double what security businesses that just do system installations are worth. Retail pharmacies with a large pool of prescriptions for drugs people take every day, like Lipitor and Lozol, command a premium over a traditional retailer because customers re-up their pills on a regular basis, creating a recurring revenue stream for the pharmacist.

Even tiny companies are worth more because of their subscription revenue. When SellabilityScore.com analyzed very small businesses with less than $500,000 in sales, we found that the average offer they attract is 2.6 times pretax profit. Compare that to the average Mosquito Squad franchise.

Mosquito Squad is a Richmond, Virginia–based company that offers to keep bugs off your patio by spraying your backyard regularly with a proprietary chemical recipe approved by the Environmental Protection Agency. Mosquito Squad franchisees target affluent home owners with an average home value north of $500,000 who entertain in their backyard and don't want to be bothered by mosquitoes.

Instead of you calling when you need them, Mosquito Squad operates on a subscription basis. You subscribe to a season of spraying, which includes 8 to 12 sprays, depending on how buggy it is where you live.

Mosquito Squad is a franchise business, and the impact of its recurring revenue model on its valuation is remarkable. According to Scott Zide, the president of Mosquito Squad's parent company, Outdoor Living Brands, Mosquito Squad franchises that changed hands over the most recent five-year period had revenue of $463,223 and sold for 3.7 times their pretax profit. That's a 42% premium over the traditional value of a company with less than $500,000 in sales, mostly because Mosquito Squad operates on a recurring subscription model and 73% of its annual spraying contracts renew each year.

Whether you plan to build a subscription-based software application or the simplest personal services business, having recurring revenue will boost the value of your most important asset.

2. The $29 Sale vs. the $4,524 Sale

The most obvious benefit of the subscription model is that it increases the lifetime value of a customer. When you sell a customer a subscription, that one sale can create a long-term relationship thanks to the magic of recurring revenue.

Let's look at an example of a typical flower store. Like many traditional businesses, the average flower store starts each month with no revenue, so they constantly have to find ways to stimulate demand. They pay for expensive retail space so they can grab your attention the day before your wedding anniversary. They buy advertising around key holidays like Mother's Day and Valentine's Day so you'll buy your flowers from them and not from the guy down the street. If they guess wrong on how many customers they will win on a given holiday, their inventory rots within a week.

Compare that model to H.Bloom, a flower company whose founders, Bryan Burkhart and Sonu Panda, say they want to become the "NetFlix of flowers."[2]

H.Bloom provides fresh-cut flowers to businesses like hotels, restaurants, and spas. Unlike traditional flower stores that have to stimulate new demand each month, it sells subscriptions to a weekly, biweekly, or monthly fresh flower delivery. Because H.Bloom doesn't need to be physically in front of potential customers, instead of paying $150 per square foot for prime retail space in Manhattan, it pays less than $30 per square foot for space on the third floor of a 100-year-old building in an industrial area of the city.

The traditional flower store sells a one-shot bouquet to a customer they may never see again, but at H.Bloom, a hotel can sign up for a weekly delivery of the basic $29 bouquet. If H.Bloom keeps the subscriber happy for three years (its monthly churn rate is less than 2%), that one $29 sale will end up creating a customer that is worth $4,524 ($29 x 156 weeks).

3. Smooth Out Demand

One of the biggest challenges in a traditional business is estimating demand. Guess high and you end up strapped for cash and with a warehouse full of inventory. Guess low and you risk running out of stock, losing out on sales and disappointing customers.

Even companies without perishable inventory are affected by

lumpy demand. Every company that employs people has to guess how much demand they will have and staff accordingly. In a people business, when you underestimate demand, your employees burn out, morale sinks, the quality of your service suffers, and your brand is damaged. If you have too many employees, they spend time gossiping about when the layoffs will come, while your profit margin shrinks because you're paying for people to sit on the bench.

By contrast, the subscription business model smoothes out demand so that you can plan your business effectively. Knowing within a few percentage points how many customers you will have next month helps ensure you have the right number of staff and adequate supplies. Optimizing your labor and raw materials means lowering your costs—and your blood pressure.

Your typical bricks-and-mortar flower store, for example, has to throw out between 30% and 50% of its flowers each month because they rot. At H.Bloom, the spoilage rate is just 2% per month.[3]

Imagine the benefits of knowing, within a few percentage points, how much revenue you're going to have next month. You could buy the right amount of raw materials and accurately plan your head count.

4. Free Market Research

Want to find out what your customers would like you to offer next? How much they would pay and what features they would insist on? You could go the traditional route of commissioning a six-figure, statistically valid telephone survey or a five-figure batch of focus groups. Alternatively, you could launch a subscription offering and get paid while you do market research.

A subscription business gives you a direct relationship with your customers and an ability to track their preferences in real time. It's why Walmart launched Goodies Co. and how Netflix knows what television series to produce or acquire next.

Take a look at subscription-based ContractorSelling.com, run by Joe Crisara. In return for a fee of $89 per month, you can subscribe and get information, tips, and advice on how to run a successful contracting business. Plumbers and electricians subscribe to Contractor Selling.com for Crisara's insight, and as they start to read articles and contribute to the forums, Crisara can see what's on his subscribers' minds.

That's important because Crisara also makes money from conferences. Seeing which articles are most popular and controversial among his members gives Crisara insight that helps when he's picking speakers and topics for his live events.

For $20 a month, Conscious Box offers a monthly selection of hand-picked, natural, GMO-free goods to try. Conscious Box asks subscribers what they think of the products in each box—and rewards them when they respond. Each product review earns 10 points, and 100 points earns the subscriber $1 to use in Conscious Box's online store.

Conscious Box then offers the manufacturers of the samples a custom online portal where marketers can see how Conscious Box subscribers rated each product. Conscious Box CEO Patrick Kelly told me that between 5% and 20% of subscribers rate each sample, giving both Conscious Box and its partners critical customer feedback.

Conscious Box uses the data to select merchandise for its online store and prominently display the products customers like best. (About 10% of Conscious Box revenue comes from online store purchases;

Kelly is looking to grow this side of his business.) Product manufacturers use the insights they gain from Kelly's panel of early-adopting, eco-friendly consumers to pick winners to sell through the company's other channels—no focus group required.

5. Get Paid Automatically

Assuming customers pay for your subscription by credit card, a subscription model means you get paid on the day you're supposed to get paid. Compare that with the typical payment cycle of a business-to-business company that sends an invoice and waits 30, 60, or 90 days for payment.

Stuart Hunt & Associates is an Edmonton-based company that safely disposes of radioactive waste. Part of its business comes from doing large cleanup jobs for massive nuclear plants and mining operations. The cash flow cycle of these large projects is horrendous. Stuart Hunt & Associates gets a purchase order from a large mining company, which allows it to start work on a project. Once it completes the job, it sends an invoice and must typically wait 120 days to get paid. In the meantime, the company still has to make payroll and keep the lights on, etc., causing cash flow stress for the owner.

The other part of the business comes from servicing the radioactive sources in small, everyday devices that are used by all kinds of organizations. You know that little wand the airport security guy assaults you with when you forget to take your watch off as you go through the X-ray machine? That has a small radioactive source inside, and to make sure it is not leaking radioactivity into unsuspecting travelers, it needs to be tested by a company like Stuart Hunt & Associates once every year.

Stuart Hunt & Associates tests thousands of radioactive devices per year. Until recently, it would send a small invoice—usually around $100—for each job. Some customers would pay on time, but most would require a follow-up phone call at the 30-day mark. Some would need a second nudge at 60 days, and each year Stuart Hunt & Associates would have to write off a few deadbeats who never paid. Given the volume of small jobs, this $6-million-per-year company employed two full-time bookkeepers, one of whom spent most of her time just collecting receivables.

Then Sean Hunt, the current president and son of founder Stuart Hunt, had an idea: Why don't we charge small customers on a recurring subscription model that bills a credit card once a year? All customers need to have their radioactive sources checked annually, so by offering a subscription service reminding customers to send in their devices, Stuart Hunt & Associates was actually simplifying the lives of its customers and getting paid faster. Now customers are charged annually before their devices are checked, improving the company's cash flow and eliminating the need to chase deadbeats for $100.

In a traditional business, you buy the raw materials, make your widget, sell it, and then collect your money. It can take months—even years—between buying the stuff you need to make your product and actually getting paid. In the subscription business, the old model is reversed. Now your customer subscribes and pays—in the case of Amazon Prime, for a full year of service—in advance.

6. Make Your Customers Sticky

Imagine that you own a 100-pound Pyrenean Mountain Dog that eats two hearty bowls of dog food a day. Feeding the love of your life is an expensive proposition, so you're always on the lookout for a deal on dog food. Once every two weeks you trudge down to the local pet supply store and cart a case of kibble home. If you see dog food on sale at your local grocery store, you'll buy it. Or if you get a coupon for a buy-one-get-one-free offer from another store, you'll take advantage of it.

Eventually, you get tired of last-minute trips to the store, so you subscribe to Warwickshire, UK–based PetShopBowl.com, which offers a Bottomless Bowl subscription service. Now you know you're going to get a shipment of dog food every two weeks, and the part of your brain that scans the flyers for dog food starts to shut down. There is no need to cart a heavy container of food back to the house every week when your shipment will arrive automatically.

Subscribers knowingly enter into an agreement in which the convenience of uninterrupted automatic service is exchanged for their future loyalty. Rather than buying once without returning, subscribers stick around—hopefully for years.

7. Subscribers Buy More

A subscription business model allows you the opportunity to talk to your customers on a regular basis as they enjoy the benefits of your subscription. This means you get an opportunity to up-sell them on products and services beyond their basic subscription.

Take, for example, the story of BirchBox, which offers a $10-

per-month subscription that delivers a collection of cosmetic and skin-care samples to your door in a beautifully wrapped box made of recycled packaging. Instead of buying the full-size version of a moisturizer, only to find it doesn't quite work for your skin type, BirchBox allows its customers (there are BirchBox programs for women and for men) to discover new products before shelling out for the big bottle.

As of August 2013, BirchBox founders Katia Beauchamp and Haley Barna were up to 400,000 subscribers and growing quickly.[4] If you're doing the math at home, that makes for almost $50 million of subscriber revenue. Not bad for a young start-up run by a couple of thirty-somethings.

But the real money for BirchBox—and the cosmetic companies who give them most of their samples to distribute for free—is in the conversion. Today, more than half of BirchBox subscribers have bought a full-size version of something they sampled from the BirchBox e-commerce site.[5]

At H.Bloom, for every $10 subscribers pay each month, the company picks up an extra $3 in one-shot orders from subscribers who add something to their order for a special occasion.

You don't need to throw away your entire business model to start a subscription service. By *adding* a subscription offering, you create a legion of customers who interact with your company each month. Every touch point represents another opportunity for you to sell more to your existing customers.

8. Recession-Proof Your Business

When you create a steady flow of recurring revenue, you insulate yourself from the worst of a potential recession.

Take a look at the transformation of New York–based Tri-State Elevator Co. The company started by installing elevators, which is the sexy part of the elevator business. When a shiny new building is built on Fifth Avenue in New York, every elevator company in the city wants to work on the job.

Most of the time Tri-State would bid on installing elevators for new buildings but lose out to larger elevator companies or manufacturers like Otis that also have an installation division. When Tri-State won a project to install an elevator in a new building, it often experienced headaches associated with delays. Big construction jobs are fraught with unknown expenses, and no matter how good Tri-State was at estimating the cost of a job, many new installation projects ended up as money losers. Gross margins on installation jobs varied from as "high" as 15% to a loss of 25%.

Then Tri-State decided to change its business model. Instead of focusing on new elevator installations for commercial properties, the company decided to focus on *maintaining* existing elevators for New York's wealthiest individuals—people who have elevators in their ultra-high-end estates, apartments, and townhomes valued between $10 and 100 million. Today Tri-State enjoys gross margins of 24% to 40% in its business of maintaining the elevators of billionaires. For a fixed monthly subscription, you can ask Tri-State to keep an eye on the private elevator in your 10,000-square-foot Manhattan penthouse. The company will inspect your elevator regularly, replace parts that are wearing out, and make its service people available to you every day of the year if an elevator gets stuck.

Now Tri-State has a steady flow of $70,000 a month in high-margin maintenance contracts, which amounts to roughly a third of its revenue each month. That steady flow of business got Tri-State through the financial crisis of 2008. In the depth of the recession, virtually all new building in New York State stopped, and it didn't restart again in a big way until 2012. If Tri-State had still been focused on chasing shiny new builds, it would have been put out of business. Its high-margin, recurring-maintenance revenue kept it going and inoculated it against the worst of the recession.

The Challenges of Adopting the Subscription Model

To be fair, there are downsides involved in moving to a subscription model. The biggest risk is spreading the cash you receive from a customer over the life of the subscription. This usually means your customers are more valuable to you over time, but in the short term, you may get less cash up front when they decide to subscribe instead of buy. But as you'll see later, there are ways to mitigate this risk and turn your subscription business into a cash spigot rather than a cash suck.

The second-biggest challenge in moving to a subscription model is getting your employees onboard. While most founders are quick to adopt a business model that is so obviously beneficial to shareholders, employees are often less interested in moving to a new way of doing things.

Employees often view themselves as having expertise in a specific industry, an expertise that they are renting to you for the time being. They see themselves first as part of an industry, and second as your employee. If they get a better offer from another company in your industry, they may leave. These employees stay stuck in traditional definitions of their industry because clinging to the industry's way of doing business reinforces their market value.

I found this out the hard way. I used to run a management-consulting company that employed a number of experienced professionals. We wooed one of our most senior consultants—I'll call him Steve—away from a brand-name consulting company. His star was on the rise in the consulting industry after several successful stints with a few of the big-name consultancies, and he was always getting headhunted.

Around this time, I made the decision to switch our consultancy to a subscription-based research business. We decided to standardize around a specific offering and develop a core set of methodologies to follow while offering our standard service on subscription.

Steve felt the standardization of our business model was going to turn our company into "McConsulting" because we were developing a systems culture like a McDonald's franchise. Steve thrived on the complexity of consulting; he tied his market value as a consultant to being able to solve the most unique challenges for his clients.

Although we paid him a salary, Steve saw himself as a freelancer whom we were merely renting. Steve wanted what was best for Steve, not our company. As a result, he resisted our move to a subscription model. He was an outspoken critic in company meetings and tried to convince junior consultants that staying with the company as it moved to a subscription model would hurt their careers.

Eventually, we parted ways with Steve. Since then I've seen many similar situations where the greatest barrier to switching to a subscription model lies within your own company. Sticking to the way your industry has always done things means you can be taken hostage by free-agent employees who hire themselves out to the highest bidder.

You may find the move to a subscription model weeds out the employees who are more loyal to your industry than to your company. While the sorting-out process can be painful in the short term, wouldn't your company be better off without these employees in the long run?

You now have my business case for building a subscription offering. Whether you plan to rethink your entire business model or just add a small annuity stream adjacent to your main business, your subscription offering will:

- Drive up the value of your company
- Increase the lifetime value of your customers
- Smooth out demand
- Cut the cost of customer market research
- Automate the collection of receivables
- Lock in your most promiscuous customers (those who are always looking for a deal and who will switch for a small price advantage)
- Trigger customers to buy a broader selection of your products and services
- Inoculate your business from the worst of a recession

Are you ready to discover your subscription model? The next section gives you an overview of nine subscription models so you can decide which one has the most potential for your business.

PART TWO

The Nine Subscription Business Models

Part Two of this book is divided into nine small chapters, each of which describes one of the nine basic subscription business models. My goal is to show that savvy companies in every industry—from restaurateurs to home builders to dance studio owners and psychologists—are creating recurring revenue streams by leveraging the subscription business model.

Not every example may seem immediately relevant to your industry. Some of the most interesting and lucrative subscription companies borrow ideas from a variety of industries or business models. As you read, I encourage you to ask the questions "How could this model apply to my industry?" and "What part of this model could I borrow for my company?"

Let's begin where the subscription model started: selling information.

CHAPTER 3

The Membership Website Model

I f you have a specific expertise or passion, no matter how obscure, there may be people willing to pay for access to what you know. The membership website subscription model involves publishing your know-how behind a paywall that requires members to buy access to your secrets.

For $129 a year, you can subscribe to the Wood Whisperer Guild, a membership website set up by Marc Spagnuolo, who shares his knowledge of woodworking with thousands of hobby cabinetmakers and enthusiasts. Sharing of specialized information via a membership website is a relatively recent phenomenon made possible by advancing technology—and is a testament to the way the public now values information.

There was a time when technology hippies thought information should be accessible to all. Stewart Brand, speaking at a 1984 Hackers Conference, reportedly used the phrase "information wants to be free."[1] Brand's quote was largely taken out of context, but it was enough to become a rallying cry for a small, noisy faction of technology activists fighting for free information online.

These people believed information was a basic right and would start online petitions the moment anyone threatened to charge for content online. One of the most public floggings was offered to the *New York Times* in 2011 when it turned on a paywall for access to content many had come to see as a public service.

The challenge with making information free is that if you take away the economic incentive to sell it, the quality of the content gets really bad. Most of us have come to our senses and understand that just like eating at a restaurant or going to the theater, good-quality things cost money to produce, and we're increasingly willing to pay for content online. Quality news organizations like the *Wall Street Journal*, the *New York Times*, and the *Financial Times* have all won hundreds of thousands of paying online subscribers, and we no longer always expect good online content to be free.

In fact, our newfound willingness to pay for information has spawned a cottage industry of membership websites. Subscribers get access to unique content, including articles, videos, webinars, and forum discussions on specialized topics.

For example, Dream of Italy is a site for people who want inside information about traveling off the beaten path in Italy. American owner Kathy McCabe grew up traveling back to her Italian homeland every year, and she developed a network of local contacts in the hospitality industry. She cultivated friendships with local farmers, restaurateurs, and boutique hotel operators. Today, she leverages this network of local contacts for a steady flow of inside information about emerging travel experiences in Italy. If the chef in Rome's best restaurant changes or a new *pensione* opens in Tuscany, Kathy is likely to know before most, and she passes this information on to her loyal subscribers, who rely on her for an insider's guide to Italy's best-kept secrets.

As it did for Kathy, the membership website model can work for your business if you have access to highly specialized information that keeps changing over time.

What Do You Know That Nobody Else Does?

If you have developed a unique approach to running your business or have been able to achieve above-average profitability in a competitive industry, then other companies in your industry want to know how you did it. The most financially successful membership websites tend to focus on helping business owners master a specific industry or skill. RestaurantOwner.com, for example, helps aspiring chefs create profitable restaurants. ContractorSelling.com helps plumbers and electricians build their companies.

MemberGate is a software platform that allows you to set up a membership website. I spoke to owner Tim Kerber, a veritable membership website guru, and asked him why business-to-business sites seem to be the most financially successful. "When it comes to their livelihood," he said, "people are much more willing to pull out their credit card."

Take, for example, DanceStudioOwner.com, the membership website of New Hampshire–based Kathy Blake. Kathy Blake has run her 900-student dance studio for 40 years. Along the way, she has been featured in *Dance Teacher* magazine and is a sought-after adviser for the members of Dance Teachers' Club of Boston and the National Dance

Council of America. In short, when it comes to running a dance studio, Kathy Blake is a national expert.

As an industry leader, she was invited to teach ballroom dancing aboard Crystal Cruises. In order to head off and teach dance on the high seas, Kathy had to figure out a way to operate her studio remotely. To help her staff cope in her absence, Kathy started writing down how she ran her successful studio so that her staff could follow her formula without her. Over time, Kathy's collection of notes, instructions, and templates grew into a comprehensive blueprint for how to run a successful dance studio.

That's when Kathy's daughter, Suzanne Blake Gerety, realized they were sitting on a valuable asset. After researching the membership website subscription business, Suzanne and Kathy decided, in 2008, to launch DanceStudioOwner.com. They would offer their insights into building a successful dance studio to subscribers, who pay $187 per year for access to their wisdom.

From 2008 to 2010, they offered charter member pricing of just $1 for the first 21 days, after which subscribers were asked to pay $97 for the full year. By 2010, Suzanne had 200 members and decided it was time to increase her price to $187 per year. Despite the doubling of the rates, the business continued to grow, offering Suzanne and Kathy a steady stream of revenue that leveled out the cyclical sales of a typical dance studio that peaks as the kids go back to school in the fall and drops off again at the end of the school year.

In the summer of 2012, Suzanne made her annual pilgrimage to the Dance Teacher Summit in New York City as an exhibitor and speaker. One of her fellow exhibitors was industry giant Revolution Dancewear. Revolution makes leotards, ballet shoes, and pretty much anything else a dancer needs to perform. It sells exclusively through dance studios and schools, the very community Suzanne and Kathy was in touch with through DanceStudioOwner.com.

Suzanne struck up a conversation with Revolution's director of marketing, and they discussed a possible partnership. After the event, Suzanne met with Robb Lippitt, the CEO of Revolution Dancewear. They discussed their shared vision for helping dance studio owners, and by the end of the meeting, Lippitt had offered to buy Dance StudioOwner.com.

Revolution Dancewear—which earned a spot on the 2013 *Inc.* 5000 list of the fastest-growing companies in the United States by posting sales of $37.2 million—wasn't interested in buying a little dance studio in New Hampshire. They wanted to buy DanceStudioOwner.com in order to insert themselves into the conversation DanceStudioOwner.com was having with thousands of dance studios each month.

Lippitt explained his acquisition rationale in his 2013 announcement of the deal:

> **This acquisition bolsters our mission, as we can now provide our customers with an outstanding online resource center for growing and succeeding in business. At the same time, it gives us deep insights into the business challenges our studio customers face every day, which ultimately will enable us to serve them better.**[2]

Just like Amazon, part of Revolution's appetite for buying smaller subscription-based companies was to gain the customer insights the company possessed. And if you need yet another reason to add a subscription offering to your existing business, consider this: Kathy Blake spent 40 years building her dance studio without ever receiving an offer to buy it. Yet five short years after she began to build a subscription business, Kathy and Suzanne's membership site was acquired by one of the giants of the dance apparel business.

Monetizing Your Members

Often a membership website can be used as entry into selling a larger-ticket item. Nobody knows more about converting subscribers into large customers than Anne Holland.

I first came to know Holland when she was the founder and owner of MarketingSherpa, an information-publishing business that indirectly competed with my subscription-based research company. After her company was acquired in 2007, she went on to run Subscription Site Insider, a website dedicated to teaching new information publishers how to set up and succeed as membership website owners. More recently, Holland founded WhichTestWon.com, which offers weekly case studies of digital-marketing programs to large enterprise customers. Thousands of subscribers see two versions of the same campaign with one slight variance (marketers call this an A/B test). WhichTestWon subscribers can test their marketing savvy by guessing which of the two campaigns had better results and then read the entire case study, which is available behind a paywall.

WhichTestWon.com subscribers pay $25 per quarter or $75 per year for a subscription. When I interviewed Holland, I asked her why the cost of the subscription was so low. "That's intentional," Holland said. "We keep the price low to get as many paying customers as we can. It's a gazillion times easier to convert a paying customer into an event attendee than it is to convince a nonpaying customer to come to an event."

And events are where Holland makes her money. Once a year, Holland hosts The Live Event (TLE) USA and TLE Europe. The retail price for a ticket to the American event is $1,895. More than 500 people attended TLE USA in 2013 to learn the latest secrets from digital marketers. In addition to delegate fees, Holland charges vendors to exhibit and sponsor the event. Through WhichTestWon.com, Holland has built trust and credibility with her subscribers. They know they're getting something of value from her, so they're more than happy to pay 20 times the cost of a subscription to attend an event.

Holland's business model for WhichTestWon comes from years of being on the frontier of the subscription economy, first by founding MarketingSherpa, which supplied case studies to marketers, and then running Subscription Site Insider, now the bible for subscription and membership site operators.

It was at MarketingSherpa that she learned the power of getting customers to buy something small as a precursor to selling them something large. MarketingSherpa used to offer its case studies for $7 each. "Everyone assumed we made tons of money from selling $7 articles," Holland told me, "but the reality is, the one-shot article business was a small part of our company." MarketingSherpa's real money-maker was the conferences. Holland employed a full-time telemarketer who called people who had ordered a $7 case study. First, the telemarketer would ensure that the customer had received the case study and then would follow up with an invitation to a live event on the same topic. "We ended up selling 900 tickets to a $1,500 conference just because we called someone who bought a $7 article."

Holland has even done testing to isolate the ideal time to upgrade a customer who has recently become a subscriber. She told me that the best response rate will always come from customers who bought something similar less than three months prior. The next-best list is those people who have bought something from you more than three months ago. The next-best list after that is people who have bought something recently from a similar company, followed finally by your registered users or people who have opted in to your e-mail updates but have never purchased. Holland explains her strategy: "In every single list testing since the 1950s, customers who have bought something similar in the last three months convert a bazillion times better than anyone else."

In summary, the membership website establishes a commercial relationship with a subscriber. While that customer can be lucrative on his own, most membership website operators use the subscription relationship as a platform to cross-sell additional things.

WHO THE MEMBERSHIP WEBSITE MODEL WORKS BEST FOR

Consider the membership website model if you have:

- A tightly defined niche market, like ambitious dance studio owners or Italy junkies or woodworking enthusiasts.

- Access to a steady flow of unique knowledge, or expertise insider information that is constantly changing and that subscribers need to stay in the know.

- Another product or service you can sell to your subscribers.

What the Insiders Say

- The most profitable membership websites are usually those of business-to-business companies that solve a real problem, offering "must have" information and maintaining constantly evolving forums that require that a subscriber stay loyal over the long term.

- Most successful operators produce a piece of content in multiple formats (e.g., video interview, podcast, and written transcript) to accommodate subscriber preferences for consuming information and increase the chances the site will be found by Google's search engine.

- It can be difficult to make a good living from just the revenue you get from subscribers alone, especially with a consumer-oriented site, so having other ways to monetize your subscribers through adjacent products and services (e.g., conferences, coaching, courses) is the best way to build a significant business around a membership website.

CHAPTER 4

The All-You-Can-Eat Library Model

Few industries have been as disrupted by technology as the music business.

Online music distribution had one of its first major breakthroughs in the year 2000 when Apple bought an MP3 player system called SoundJam. Apple evolved the software into iTunes, which debuted with the first iPod in the fall of 2001.

In 2003, Apple launched iTunes 4, the first version of the software to feature the iTunes Music Store. It was also the first edition to be available on Microsoft Windows, opening up iTunes to PC users. "Consumers don't want to be treated like criminals, and artists don't want their valuable work stolen," Apple cofounder Steve Jobs said in a statement at the time. "The iTunes Music Store offers a groundbreaking solution for both."[1]

Over the next six years, iTunes became the Internet's record store, eventually peaking at a whopping 69% share of U.S. music sales in 2009. But lately that market dominance has started to falter. By 2013, iTunes's share of online music sales had started to decline, and it ended the year around 63%.

But it is not the drop in music sales that worries iTunes. A far more insidious threat is that consumers no longer want to buy their music at all. Lately we've taken to renting our music through subscriptions to companies like Spotify, Rdio, and Rhapsody. Ted Cohen, the former digital chief for the record label EMI Music, told *Bloomberg Business-week*: "It's no longer about individual tracks; it's about access. The concept of buying music at 99 cents a song is becoming irrelevant."[2]

To compete against subscription-based music services, Apple launched iTunes Radio in the fall of 2013. It was launched as an advertiser-supported, free service (iTunes Match subscribers get the ad-free version). The story of online music is still being written, but one thing is for sure: the subscription model has disrupted it forever.

The all-you-can-eat library subscription model offers unlimited access to a warehouse of value. Like any library, you'll never consume all of the information available, but the breadth of content that is offered promises to always have something you like. The business model is simple: the provider accumulates a wide selection of content, and the consumer rents access to it.

Take, for example, the subscription business Ancestry.com. For around $20 a month, you can rent access to a library of content that can help you piece together your family tree. Ancestry.com invests heavily in acquiring and digitizing historical information on behalf of its subscribers. In one large-scale effort, Ancestry.com spent $3 million to acquire more than 90 million U.S. war records from the first English settlement at Jamestown in 1607 through the Vietnam War's end in 1975.[3] The treasure trove included 37 million images, draft registration cards from both world wars, military yearbooks, prisoner-of-war records from four wars, unit rosters from the Marine Corps from 1893 through 1958, and Civil War pension records, among other data.

Uploading the records took almost a year and required the help of some 1,500 handwriting specialists, who invested 270,000 hours to review the documents.[4] While the effort would have been prohibitive for any one individual, the cost to acquire, analyze, and digitize the records was spread out over Ancestry's 2-million-plus paying subscribers.

The all-you-can-eat library model works well for Netflix and has disrupted the old movie rental business, knocking companies like Blockbuster off its pedestal. Other examples include GameFly (video games); Entitle, which was launched as eReatah, and Oyster (e-books); and Lynda.com (how-to courses).

Acquiring Your Buffet

Given the challenge of creating a large library of content before you have a single paying subscriber, you may be tempted to think the all-you-can-eat library model is best suited for media giants and venture-capital-backed start-ups. However, with some creativity and a little cash, anyone can assemble a library of content and rent access to it. That's what happened with Huntington Beach, California–based New Masters Academy.

Back in 2012, Joshua Jacobo, a 28-year-old artist, couldn't believe the cost of a good art education. Major universities and colleges were charging from $10,000 to $100,000 for an art degree. "Students were paying a ton of money and getting third-string teachers," Jacobo told me.

In addition to the cost of a good art education, Jacobo explained that access to art education was severely limited by geography.

Jacobo set out to "democratize art education" by putting together a library of how-to classes led by real artists. Each class would be streamed live via video from the New Masters Academy website. Jacobo began by charging $19 a month (it's now up to $29) for access to all of his content.

He had only one problem: he had no content.

Jacobo was bootstrapping his start-up with $70,000 of his own money, and he didn't have enough cash to acquire a big library of existing content, so instead he invited individual artists to partner with him to build the site. The artists were asked to give their time to teach a lesson and let Jacobo and his team record a video. New Masters Academy then edited the video and posted it to its site. The artist was paid a commission based on how many subscribers the site generated. Now, each month New Masters Academy takes a portion of its revenue and slices off a chunk for its instructors. The instructors divvy up the pool of cash proportionally based on the amount of content uploaded. The more hours of teaching they have uploaded, the bigger the slice of the commission pie they receive.

This innovative formula for acquiring content allowed Jacobo to launch the site with 100 hours of video content instantly available. By early 2014, New Masters Academy was up to 2,000 subscribers and 350 hours of video lessons. Jacobo's subscribers come from all over the world, including Egypt, China, Japan, Russia, and the United States. He was able to build his company without going outside for venture-capital cash, resulting in a site that was cash flow positive after its first month of operation.

Like the membership website model, the best way to win subscribers for your all-you-can-eat library model is to invite them to share in content they care about—and then ask them to subscribe for more.

In the case of New Masters Academy, Jacobo set up a Facebook fan page where he posted his art and that of his instructors for free, building a vibrant community of art lovers. In eight months, Jacobo built a legion of 30,000 Facebook fans. When he launched New Masters Academy, he quickly converted more than 1,000 of his Facebook fans into paying subscribers.

According to Don Nicholas, CEO of the publishing consultancy Mequoda Group, LLC, Jacobo's experience is common. Over the years, Nicholas has tested virtually every combination of sales tactics you can imagine to get people to pay for a subscription, and he has found the winning formula to be a two-step approach: first, get unique visitors to your website to opt in to a relationship with your company by subscribing to an e-mail newsletter (or joining a Facebook fan page, Twitter feed, etc.), then convert opt-ins to paying subscribers through a sales funnel.

Each year Mequoda tracks publishing industry conversion benchmarks. In 2013 the average publisher in its survey pool was able to convert 3.2% of its monthly unique visitors into free e-mail newsletter subscribers. Of the registered e-mail subscribers, publishers were able to convert between 3% and 30% into paying customers of some kind. The largest determinant of where you will land on the conversion scale is how many subscriptions and products you offer. If all you have is one paid subscription offer, you're likely to be on the lower end of the scale, whereas if you have hundreds of products and subscriptions available, you might expect to convert more visitors into subscribers. Note that Jacobo's experience at New Masters Academy, where he converted roughly 3% of his Facebook fans into paying customers, falls neatly into the lower end of Nicholas's range for information publishers. As Jacobo increases the breadth of New Masters Academy's offerings, he's likely to see a corresponding increase in the proportion of his Facebook fans who convert into paying customers.

WHO THE ALL-YOU-CAN-EAT LIBRARY MODEL WORKS BEST FOR

Consider the all-you-can-eat library model if you have:

- A library of "evergreen" content—or the wherewithal to acquire one. Netflix owns the rights to more than 100,000 movies and television shows for its streaming subscription. Even the most couch-addicted teenager could not consume the entire library, especially since new movies and original content are added regularly, which means that there is always a reason to keep up your subscription.

- A legion of existing fans (blog subscribers, Twitter followers, LinkedIn connections, etc.) who already consume your free content.

What the Insiders Say

- Successful all-you-can-eat library model operators sprinkle just enough new content into the offering to keep subscribers loyal while relying on a large library of "evergreen" content as the foundation of membership.

- To prevent subscribers from cherry-picking the best parts of your library, it may be necessary to give customers an ultimatum: subscribe to the entire library or you can't access any of it.

- The acquisition of your library is a chicken-or-egg conundrum. Unless you have a truckload of money, look for creative ways to partner (e.g., licensing, revenue-sharing agreements) with content owners to build a library that's large enough to impress subscribers.

CHAPTER 5

The Private Club Model

I t's 7:00 a.m. on a warm February morning in Melbourne, Australia. Given the forecasted heat of the day ahead, you have opted for pleated, knee-length shorts, but right about now, you're feeling a little self-conscious, having hiked your socks halfway up your calf to comply with club rules.

After 10 years on the waiting list, you've arrived and are partaking of the rarefied atmosphere of the Royal Melbourne Golf Club (RMGC), where only members—properly dressed ones, that is—are welcome. RMGC consistently draws in members by not only offering fantastic facilities, including two world-class, 18-hole courses (the west course has been ranked number one in Australia and is frequently listed in the top 20 courses worldwide), but also by offering more than just golf. After waiting more than a decade for membership and paying thousands of dollars in initiation fees, you haven't just purchased a future of great golf, you've purchased access to a private club, which means the opportunity to rub shoulders with fellow members who can afford the $3,500-per-year membership fee.[1]

The private club model offers subscribers ongoing access to something rare. While it is most commonly associated with exclusive sports clubs—think golf, tennis, skiing, yachting—it is also used by businesses selling to other businesses. A large part of the value of the private club model is not only accessing that which is rare but also the chance to meet with a network of other people who—like you—made the cut.

Who, Rather than What

Consider the story of Joe Polish. Polish started his career as a humble carpet cleaner. He learned how to build a successful carpet cleaning company and then began teaching those lessons to other carpet cleaners. He broadened his reach to all industries by publishing, in a set of multiple audio CDs, *Piranha Marketing System: The Seven Success Multiplying Factors to Dominate Any Market You Enter*, one of Nightingale Conant's best-selling training programs for entrepreneurs keen to learn about marketing.

Joe Polish now runs Genius Network, a networking organization that, in exchange for an annual investment of $25,000, invites entrepreneurs, authors, and innovators to meet three times a year to share ideas. "It's kind of like a wisdom network," Polish told me. "It's where you find people who have incredible wisdom and you share that."

Just like buying a membership in RMGC, investing in Genius Network is a decision you make with both the rational and the emotional sides of your brain. As any Porsche salesmen will tell you, exclusive things are bought on emotion and justified with logic.

For the logical side of your decision making, Polish offers two meetings per year at his headquarters in Arizona, plus an annual event at an exclusive location to attract members to Genius Network. Polish also appeals to the emotional side of your brain because at least half of the value proposition of joining Polish's group is *who* you'll meet rather than *what* you'll learn. Polish sells prospective members using reams of what he calls "social proof," like interviews with happy and successful members describing what they get out of the network and pictures of Polish with entrepreneurs like Richard Branson and Bill Gates.

Polish isn't shy about his value proposition. "This is the group of people you would want access to in your 'dream rolodex,'" he says. Polish is careful to cultivate an air of exclusivity around his subscription. That exclusivity is what makes this private club model so appealing. As he puts it, "When there is more demand than supply, everyone wants to buy."

Barriers to Entry

One of the things that makes the private club model work is the privacy itself. For some achievement-oriented people, the higher you make the barrier to enter, the more they want to climb over it.

Look at TIGER 21, which stands for The Investment Group for Enhanced Results in the 21st Century, the world's most exclusive investment club. Members pay a $30,000-per-year subscription fee; globally, the group has approximately 200 members who collectively manage roughly $20 billion in assets. To get into this private club, you need a minimum of $10 million in investable assets.[2]

TIGER 21 members meet monthly in small regional groups of about a dozen members each. Once the meeting starts, mobile phones are turned off, doors are closed to outsiders, and the members get down to business. At the center of every meeting is the Portfolio Defense—a one-hour presentation from a member who is asked to reveal the intimate details of his portfolio so that the other members can critique his investment approach.

Asking high-net-worth investors, successful entrepreneurs, and captains of industry to reveal the intimate details of their financial lives is not easy, but it works for TIGER 21 because the Portfolio Defense is a requirement of all members. Further, because each member has crossed the threshold of wealth required for membership, there is mutual respect within the group.

Subscribing for Status

In some ways, the private club model sells social status—think of it as social climbing on subscription.

One of the best examples of subscribing for status is the rise of the luxury vacation "destination club." The idea of a destination club was introduced in 1998, when Rob McGrath, a veteran of the timeshare development business, created a club called Private Retreats. McGrath's concept was simple: target affluent families who want the benefits of second-home ownership without the cost or the downside of being forced to go back to the same place year after year.

One of the largest and most successful destination clubs is Exclusive

Resorts, started in 2002 by brothers Brent and Brad Handler. AOL founder Steve Case bought majority ownership of Exclusive Resorts in 2003 and expanded the concept.

Instead of buying a 3,500-square-foot vacation home in Maui for $3 million, you can simply join Exclusive Resorts and get access to a portfolio of equally impressive digs in return for your annual subscription. Exclusive Resorts offers a few packages; the basic offering in 2014 combined a onetime membership fee of $170,000 with annual dues of around $1,150 per day for 20 days per year during which you have access to club properties. You get to entertain your family and friends at a mind-blowing home for a fraction of the cost of actually owning and maintaining it.

Businesses Also Subscribe for Status

The subscribe for status idea is not limited to attracting consumers to your subscription; it works in B2B as well, when businesses want to portray an image that allows them to punch above their weight class.

There was a time when successful companies would buy a vacation property in the business's name in order to reward key employees and woo potential executive hires. You knew you had made it when the boss handed you the keys to the holiday house and insisted you take your spouse away for the weekend.

Today, businesses want to reward employees and portray an image of success without having to cough up the dough for a million-dollar mansion. Destination club Inspirato launched Inspirato for Business, which offers vacation property licenses to small and mid-size companies that compete with Fortune 500 giants for key employees. For a onetime initiation of $15,000 plus a $20,000-a-year subscription, a business can buy an Enterprise license, which entitles them to an Inspirato account manager, a dedicated trip planner, and on-site concierges in each destination, plus a branded web portal so employees and their spouses can remember your company's generosity as they make their arrangements for a reward trip.

Could It Work in Your Industry?

As with all the subscription models I'm presenting in this book, I encourage you not to say "that would never work in my industry," but to keep asking the questions "How could this model apply to my industry?" and "What part of this model could I borrow for my company?" Those are questions restaurant owner Roberto Martella is happy he asked himself back in 2004.

Martella owns an upscale restaurant in North Toronto called Grano. The competition for the dining dollar of affluent Torontonians is stiff, so in 2004 Martella and friends Rudyard Griffiths and Patrick Luciani decided to do something novel. They launched the Grano Speaker Series (now called the Salon Speaker Series) and invited big-name speakers, such as economist Paul Volcker, to come to the restaurant and give short, unscripted speeches.

Martella's restaurant has 300 seats, and bringing in A-list speakers is expensive. So he and his partners decided to structure the series as a subscription business. Well-heeled bankers and lawyers are invited every quarter to hear a private speech from some of the biggest thinkers in the world for an annual subscription of $1,200.

The series has since expanded beyond Toronto to three other cities. Each event is held in a small venue that gives subscribers unusually close access to renowned speakers like Malcolm Gladwell and Bob Woodward.

As it's a private club with elite memberships, at least part of the value is being able to rub shoulders with fellow subscribers, every one a bigwig, in a private space.

WHO THE PRIVATE CLUB MODEL WORKS BEST FOR

Consider the private club model if you have:

- Something that's in limited supply—almost always a service or an experience—and in high demand among affluent consumers.

- A market of achievement-oriented "strivers," who are always attracted to the greener grass on the other side.

What the Insiders Say

- The secret to making the private club model work is *not* offering à la carte access. Force customers to make a decision: if they want access to something truly rare, the only way they can have it is by entering into a long-term relationship. You can't buy a Portfolio Defense from TIGER 21; you have to join.

- The greatest strength of the private club model is also its biggest weakness. By definition, what you're selling is in limited supply. There are only so many people with $10 million of liquid wealth, so there will always be an inherent limit to how big TIGER 21 can grow without lowering its membership criteria, which would dilute the value proposition. When members have trouble booking a tee time at RMGC because the club has accepted too many new golfers, old members get grumpy.

CHAPTER 6

The Front-of-the-Line Model

Imagine you've decided to take your family on a vacation to Atlanta. There are two ways to manage your trip. You could do what most people do and stand in the long lines at the busy tourist attractions that cater to families on summer vacation; or you could lubricate the whole trip and buy your way to the front of practically every line you see.

When you get to the airport, you could stand in line at the regular check-in counter, or you could skip the queue and, assuming you have one of those premium-priced credit cards, use the business-class check-in desk for your flight. You can flash your fancy card again to be whisked off to a special security line.

When you arrive at your hotel, you can go right to the gold-level check-in counter in recognition of what you spend with the chain each year.

In the morning, you decide to take the kids to Six Flags Over

Georgia amusement park and hop on the I-85. You could sit in traffic with the rest of the commuters, but you planned ahead and bought a Pay n Go Peach Pass, which allows you to jump into a dedicated lane for drivers who have purchased access to less traffic.

Once at Six Flags, you could simply buy your day pass to the park. But it's July and your kids are keen to try all the rides, so you cough up the cash for each member of your family to have the $45 gold-level FLASH Pass, which cuts your wait time for rides in half.

It's noon on your first day of your summer holiday and you have already spent hundreds of dollars to jump to the front of the line in five different queues and in exchange improved the vacation experience for your family.

The front-of-the-line subscription model involves selling priority access to a group of your customers. The model was popularized by the software industry but can be used by any company with customers willing to pay to jump the service queue.

Doubling Down on the Subscription Model

Salesforce.com is a subscription business that provides software that sales teams use to manage their contacts online. The company has doubled its bet on the subscription business model by also offering subscription-based service packs they call Success Plans. At Salesforce .com, everyone gets basic-level support: you submit a ticket through the online system, and someone will provide you with an e-mail response within two business days.

If you want a response to your concern faster than two business days, you can buy an enhanced service package on a subscription basis. The least-expensive paid service package, called Premiere, gives subscribers a phone number to call to get issues resolved and a one-hour turnaround time on what Salesforce.com deems to be "mission critical" problems.[1]

If a few minutes of downtime would equate to a lot of lost revenue for your business, you can buy Salesforce.com's most expensive service package, called Mission Critical Success, which will get you a response on critical outages within 15 minutes.[2]

When you adopt the front-of-the-line subscription model, you are publicly declaring that all of your customers are *not* treated equally. That may sound wrong, but prioritizing some customers over others is something most of us do unconsciously every day. Think back to the last time your largest customer called to complain about an issue. Did you prioritize her call over that of a small customer?

Most people understand that businesses prioritize their customers and will understand as long as you explain how you prioritize.

With the front-of-the-line subscription model you're being transparent about who gets served first, which in some ways is fairer than deprioritizing some customers without telling them why.

Not Just for Software Companies

Software companies like Salesforce.com may have popularized the front-of-the-line subscription model, but you don't need to be a technology company to sell access to the front of the line.

Take a look at Boston-based Thriveworks. The company offers a program in which, for $99 a year, you get access to a personal counselor or coach who will meet with you within 24 hours to discuss whatever you want to talk about. If you're struggling with depression or addiction, or just want someone to discuss a major life decision with, Thriveworks subscribers are only ever 24 hours away from a counseling session. If the issue is more urgent, Thriveworks subscribers have 24/7 phone access to an on-call mental health expert. Thriveworks also offers an "ask a coach" program in which subscribers can send in any coaching-related question and get a written answer from a Thriveworks provider within 24 hours.

That's a big improvement over the wait time in a regular counselor's office where you can wait days for a counselor to call back and weeks before you get in to see a therapist. When you're dealing with mental health and critical life decisions, time counts, which is one reason Anthony Centore started Thriveworks.

In 2008, Centore moved to Cambridge, Massachusetts, to work as a counselor for a local practice. Within four months of Centore's arrival, the practice went out of business. Trying to understand why it failed, Centore analyzed how its customers were treated. He discovered that some customers had had to wait days before anyone from the office would return their calls. Patients—many in crisis—were often being asked to wait weeks for a face-to-face meeting with a counselor.

Centore knew that it is hard enough to call a therapist for help, so when patients muster the courage to reach out, they need to talk to someone right away. If patients call and get voice mail, rather than leave a message, many are likely to try to deal with the situation themselves—sometimes with catastrophic results.

Centore called some other counselors in town to see how long it would take him to get an appointment. He called 40 counselors and was sent to voice mail 40 times. He realized there was a market for a concierge-like system for people dealing with issues like depression and addiction or couples who need counseling.

By early 2014, Thriveworks was collecting several million dollars of annual revenue and had offices in 11 locations in the United States. Like many of the subscription models in this book, the $99 subscription Thriveworks customers pay each year accounts for only about 20% of the company's revenue. The other 80% comes from payments collected by Thriveworks' counselors from customers and their insurance companies for their appointments.

To offer a front-of-the-line subscription, you'll need to think through how you plan to handle customers who pay for a special service queue.

For example, if you offer online support through an application like Zendesk or Desk.com, you can easily route your subscribers to the front of the queue. Most such applications allow you to flag customers of a certain type and prioritize their cases. If your customers deal with you in person, you might consider setting up a dedicated reception area similar to the way Home Depot gives contractors their own service counter or your local bank offers business customers a special teller window.

If your customers interact with you over the phone, you can set up a dedicated call center for your subscribers or a special number for subscribers to call. You could also use a "follow the sun" strategy in which you set up service employees based in different time zones so there is always someone available to speak live with a customer, no matter what time of the day or night they call.

What would your customers pay to cut your standard service line and jump right to the front? Could you charge your customers a small monthly fee for peace of mind, for knowing that when they have an issue they will be taken care of first? It may seem like an inconsequential amount of money, but a small fee paid by a large enough group of your customers can add a steady stream of recurring revenue that will help provide a base of sales each month, boost cash flow, and make your company more valuable when it is time to sell.

WHO THE FRONT-OF-THE-LINE MODEL WORKS BEST FOR

Consider the front-of-the-line model if you have:

- A relatively complex product or service.

- Customers who are not overly price sensitive.

- Customers for whom waiting in line can have catastrophic consequences.

What the Insiders Say

- A front-of-the-line subscription model can be used in conjunction with other subscription models to add an additional annuity stream of recurring revenue.

- To use this subscription model, it's important that you already have a good reputation for baseline service. If your customers have been satisfied with your basic service, they can reasonably assume that paying for the next tier up will wow them.

- Leverage technology and systems (e.g., Zendesk or a dedicated phone number staffed by experienced support staff) so that you don't lump your standard customers in with those who are paying for a special tier of service.

- The front-of-the-line subscription model can work doubly well when your customers are small and mid-size businesses that lack their own in-house resources to get their questions answered. Apple's Joint Venture subscription offering is designed for small companies that do not have a full-time IT person on-site, so the prospect of training staff on a new system is daunting.

CHAPTER 7

The Consumables Model

These next two chapters profile subscription models in the growing category of subscription-based e-commerce. These companies offer a product rather than a service on a subscription basis. Unlike software or service providers, subscription-based e-commerce companies have the added complexity of acquiring a supply of whatever it is they sell and then dealing with the logistics headache of shipping the product to subscribers.

I call the first of the two the consumables model. It involves offering a subscription to a product that the customer needs to replenish on a regular basis. The value proposition is simple: life is too short to worry about mundane tasks like remembering to pick up diapers or razor blades. Subscribe and you'll never run out.

Mark Levine and Michael Dubin first met at a party in 2010. The two started lamenting the cost of buying razor blades. Levine, who has a background in manufacturing and product development, said he knew where to get replacement blades in bulk—cheaply.

In January 2011, they had started work on the company that would become Dollar Shave Club, whose subscribers get replacement razor blades sent to their door on a regular schedule. By July 2011 they had built a website and were offering a basic subscription service for good-quality replacement razor blades. Dubin worked his media connections and managed to get their first thousand subscribers by the end of 2011. But the business really took off after they made their first YouTube video in 2012. The video is a hilarious introduction to the company, featuring cofounder Dubin rallying men tired of overpaying for replacement razor blades. The video attracted so much attention that it crashed Dollar Shave Club's servers. Within 48 hours of the video's release, the company received 12,000 orders.[1] Dubin set about assembling an army of friends and contractors to fulfill orders for his new subscribers.

Dubin described the chaos to the *New York Times*:

> **In the beginning, we were printing a shipping label every 5 to 10 seconds. That might sound fast, but it's not when you need to print thousands and thousands of them. We had no inventory tracking system so we were using Post-it notes and binders to keep track of who we sent razors to and when. It was all so labor-intensive. But it was our early staffers that helped us turn the corner. We have since moved our warehouse and fulfillment to a third-party logistics center in Kentucky where our orders are packed and fulfilled automatically.**

By June 2014, Dollar Shave Club had grown to 40 employees

serving 330,000 subscribers, and the legendary video had been viewed almost 15 million times.[2]

Fifteen years before Levine and Dubin first met, Samy Liechti was experimenting with the consumables model in creating his "sockscription" brand. Liechti, along with his partner at the time, Marcel Roth, is the founder of Zurich-based Blacksocks, a company that will ship subscribers a new set of black dress socks every few months. Liechti got the idea for a sock subscription back in 1994, when he was a young, hotshot advertising executive eager to impress a group of Japanese executives. After a business dinner, the group retired to a Japanese teahouse, where it is customary to remove one's shoes. Liechti slipped off his loafers to reveal a mismatched pair of tired black socks, one of which exposed his big toe emerging from the fraying fabric. In his haste to prepare for the dinner, Liechti had grabbed an old, worn-out pair of socks. Liechti survived the embarrassment but came home with a business idea—no one would ever have to suffer the indignity of worn-out socks again.

Today, Blacksocks has approximately 30,000 subscribers around the world who receive a regular shipment of black socks for around $100 a year. Each pair of socks is identical, so you never have to worry about searching for a matching pair in the bottom of the dryer.

Both Dollar Shave Club and Blacksocks have overcome their initial logistics and fulfillment hiccups to grow their subscriber bases—but they could be in for more trouble ahead.

The Everything Subscription

The biggest challenge facing consumables subscription companies like Dollar Shave Club and Blacksocks is how to differentiate their offerings from what big online retailers like Amazon and Walmart can offer. At last count, Amazon has or is building 40 massive distribution centers across the United States so it can economically deliver on its promise of shipping thousands of goods to Amazon Prime customers in two days for free.[3] Amazon also offers Subscribe & Save on virtually all of its consumable products—which is the equivalent of saying that almost all consumable products are now available via an Amazon subscription.

Just offering a subscription is no longer a differentiating value proposition, and if Amazon (or Target or Walmart) sees you getting traction selling a generic product or service it has access to, you won't last long as an independent company. Most companies will be squashed, and the remaining few will be pressured into selling to one of the mega retailers or e-tailers: *let us buy you or we'll put you out of business.* Just take a look at the circumstances surrounding Amazon's acquisition of Diapers.com.

Marc Lore and Vinit Bharara started Diapers.com in 2005 to give sleep-deprived parents an easy way to schedule recurring shipments of diapers, wipes, and all the other consumables you need to care for a baby. Unlike Dollar Shave Club, Diapers.com wasn't shy about revealing the original supplier of the diapers. The company was offering the same Huggies Little Snugglers and Pampers Swaddlers that moms could buy from Amazon.

The business grew quickly and caught the attention of Amazon, which sent Jeff Blackburn to visit with Lore and Bharara. According to *Bloomberg Businessweek*'s Brad Stone, the author of *The Everything Store: Jeff Bezos and the Age of Amazon*, Blackburn was a senior vice president of business development for Amazon, which means he was in charge of buying companies for Jeff Bezos. According to Stone, Blackburn told Lore and Bharara that Amazon was getting ready to invest in the diapers category and they should think hard about selling to Amazon.[4]

Soon after meeting with Blackburn, Lore and Bharara saw Amazon drop its prices on diapers by 30%. They assumed Amazon was intentionally trying to undercut them, so they manipulated the price of diapers, moving the price up and down and watched as Amazon prices changed in lockstep.

As Amazon started to exert more of its clout on the pricing of diapers, Diapers.com started to feel the pinch. Its revenue stalled, and the venture capitalists that had backed Lore and Bharara balked at financing a price war with Amazon. Feeling the pinch, Lore and Bharara flew to Seattle to discuss the possibility of being acquired by Amazon.

While Lore and Bharara were with Amazon executives, Amazon released word to the media that it was launching Amazon Mom, a service that offered free two-day shipping on diapers, with an additional 30% off already discounted diapers for those who signed up for a Subscribe & Save recurring shipment of diapers. Reading the news reports, Diapers.com employees tried frantically to reach Lore and Bharara to discuss how they should react to the threat of Amazon Mom. But the founders were not answering their phones. They were in a boardroom at Amazon headquarters discussing the sale of their company.

On November 8, 2010, Amazon announced it had purchased Quidsi Inc., the parent company of Diapers.com, for $500 million.[5] "I'm not sure which is more unpleasant—changing diapers, paying too much for them, or running out of them," said Jeff Bezos, founder and CEO of Amazon.com. "This acquisition brings together two companies who are committed to providing great prices and fast delivery to parents, making one of the chores of being a parent a little easier and less expensive."

Diapers.com was one of the lucky ones. It had built a $300-million-a-year business before Amazon decided it wanted to enter the space. Given its head start, it made sense for Amazon to buy Diapers.com and get immediate scale. But for every Diapers.com, there are likely a thousand subscription businesses that fail to differentiate what their business has to offer and instead rely on price to try to compete in a battle Amazon is likely to win every time.

Your Best Defense: Branding

So is it possible for a small business to succeed with the consumables model? Yes, provided you build brand equity and guard your supply chain.

Amir Elaguizy is one of the leading pioneers of the subscription-based e-commerce movement. He is the founder of Cratejoy, a subscription-based e-commerce platform that companies like Conscious Box use to run their businesses. When I spoke with him, Elaguizy elaborated on the importance of building a brand for companies leveraging the consumables model: "The guys who are going to be around in ten years are not just hawking other people's products. The companies that will survive have two things in common: they care deeply about the product, and they are focused on building a brand."

Building a unique brand requires that your positioning meet two criteria: it needs to be important to customers *and* make you unique. In virtually every product category with potential, Amazon has already locked out the two most obvious ways to differentiate your subscription because Amazon will almost always be cheaper and faster when comparing apples to apples. That leaves only a few possibilities for differentiating your consumables subscription.

Dollar Shave Club is not just selling cheap blades. Levine and Dubin are building a brand that's defined by having a little fun. You can see that in their product lineup: you can choose from a basic two-blade razor they call the Humble Twin or a four-blade model they describe as the Lover's Blade; you can go all the way up to the six-blade, top-of-the-line offering called the Executive.

Unlike the market leaders who use traditional distribution channels to sell blades with more clinical names, such as Fusion ProGlide and Schick Hydro 5, Dollar Shave Club is building a human brand guys can relate to.

"Tech start-ups often focus on functionality," Dubin said at a 2013 industry event in Ireland, "but we've had a lot of success building an emotional brand."

While the consumables model may sound easy, building a brand and investing in the technology and fulfillment infrastructure to serve hundreds of thousands of subscribers is expensive, which is why Dubin and Levine have had to share the Dollar Shave Club pie with a lot of outside investors. In October 2013, Dollar Shave Club announced it had raised $12 million in a series B round of funding, following a $9.8 million series A round that itself was preceded by a $1 million seed round.[6]

Like Dollar Shave Club, Blacksocks is building a brand as well. In Europe, Blacksocks is a more established brand, having won a number of quality awards, including top scores from both *Kassensturz* and *K-Tipp*, publications similar to *Consumer Reports* magazine in the United States. I spoke with Lori Rosen, the Blacksocks U.S.-based managing partner, who discussed the company's marketing strategy. "We sell on quality and convenience," said Rosen. "Our socks are high quality and made in Italy."

When it comes to consumables, if you're not going to build a brand, the best customer experience is invisible. Unlike subscribing to BirchBox.com, where part of the fun is in discovering new cosmetic samples in your monthly box, shopping for a consumables product offers no inherent enjoyment. It's not like buying a car, where you get to slide into a beautiful leather seat and inhale the new-car smell. You're buying a commodity, and if you're not going to offer a branded experience, then the fastest, least painful option always wins.

Control the Product

A big part of building a brand is controlling the product itself. In Dollar Shave Club's case, it doesn't manufacturing the blades. Instead, *CBS MarketWatch* reports, it buys the four- and six-blade options from Dorco, a South Korean company with a San Diego–based U.S. subsidiary.[7]

You won't see the Dorco brand name splashed on the outside of a Dollar Shave Club box. Why would Dollar Shave Club be shy about revealing the manufacturer of its blades? It comes down to building a brand. If customers see Dollar Shave Club as just a middleman hawking a commodity blade they can buy elsewhere, consumers will be inclined to price-shop competitors. By contrast, if you want to buy the Lover's Blade, there is only one place that offers it—and you have to subscribe to get it.

Amazon, Walmart, and Target do product selection and speed of delivery better than most of us. As the big e-tailers offer more of their consumables on subscription, you need to offer the customer another reason to buy from you.

The more we believe a product is unique and offers a better experience, the more the provider has the leeway to set his own price. That's why some people pay double for a T-shirt with a Nike swoosh—they have fallen in love with the brand and believe their choice of T-shirt says a little something about them. It's the same reason many of us buy Coke at the grocery store when a generic cola is half the price.

For a consumables subscription model to work in the long term, you need something other than price and selection to compete against the big players.

WHO THE CONSUMABLES MODEL WORKS BEST FOR

Consider the consumables model if you have:

- Something to sell consumers that naturally runs out.

- Something to offer that is annoying to replenish.

What the Insiders Say

- To compete with Amazon (and the other big-box e-tailers) you need to brand what you sell as your own. Name the product yourself, even if you're buying it from a supplier.

- Invite customers to fall in love with your brand through the experience you provide. When big e-tailers can win on clinical points like price, delivery speed, and breadth of product selection, you need to give customers a different reason to choose you.

- Make sure you have a steady flow of supply. Either take control of the manufacturing process or ensure you can find enough supply when you need it.

- Don't underestimate the logistical challenges involved in fulfilling orders for a physical product or in providing service for thousands of subscribers.

CHAPTER 8

The Surprise Box Model

The second form of subscription-based e-commerce that companies leverage is the surprise box model. This model involves shipping a curated package of goodies to your subscribers each month. As the name suggests, part of the fun for the customer is discovering a new set of products each month. For example, if you're an endurance sports nut, you can get a JackedPack full of a new batch of sports gels and workout supplements delivered monthly. If you need to spice up your love life, you can subscribe to SpicySubscriptions.com and get a box full of new lovemaking paraphernalia each month. And if you need to upgrade your style, you can subscribe to StitchFix and receive five new clothing items and accessories per month based on your preferences.

Such boxes are typically built around a theme users feel passionate about. These days, there are few things many people feel more fanatical about than the family dog. According to fad watcher TrendHunter.com, one of the fastest-growing trends in United States is the humanization of pets.[1] Which is something Henrik Werdelin, Carly Strife, and Matt Meeker are exploiting in their company BarkBox.

In return for a $20-a-month subscription, BarkBox will send you a curated box of treats, toys, and accessories for your dog. The company describes its target market as "dog parents," not simply dog owners. "Owners own their pet," says Matt Meeker, one of the founders of BarkBox. "Dog parents: it's a member of the family."[2]

There are obviously a lot of dog parents in the world because between 2012 and 2013 BarkBox grew tenfold. By April 2014 nearly 200,000 subscribers were forking over about $20 a month in the name of their dog.

BarkBox articulates the surprise box promise on its website: "Each month is thoughtfully crafted together and each item unique from anything we'll ever send in a later box—variety is the spice of life, no?"[3]

The Curator

A big part of the value these subscription companies provide is curation, which has become increasingly important as Google has made choice infinite. Today, virtually any product is an Internet search away, but there is no safeguard to ensure you are buying a good-quality product from a reputable supplier. In the case of BarkBox, at least part of the value proposition is that it screens out bad products that are not fit for your pet. All its dog treats come from suppliers based in the United States or Canada; none of the products include rawhide or anything processed with formaldehyde.[4]

Before Google, the vetting of products was largely done by department-store buyers, who would consider hundreds of products a year and select only the very best for their customers. Nowadays, we don't shop in department stores as much, but consumers still want someone to go to the trouble of testing what is available to ensure it stands up to the marketer's claim.

When Unique Is the Enemy of Available

Standard Cocoa is another New York City–based start-up, founded in 2012 by Jordana Kava and Bernard Klein. Leveraging the surprise box model, Standard Cocoa set a goal of connecting people who love chocolate with those who make it.

Kava hatched the idea for Standard Cocoa while working for the global chocolate brand Godiva. She noticed that small-craft chocolate makers had virtually no chance of competing against global giants like Godiva and more mainstream brands like Ghirardelli and Lindt, which had retail distribution in drug and grocery stores locked up.

Kava decided to launch a subscription service that offered a curated box of chocolates from craft chocolate makers around the world. For around $25 a month, Standard Cocoa will send a box of goodies to your doorstep. Each Standard Cocoa box comes complete with a history of the featured chocolate maker so subscribers understand the company's backstory and how it plies its craft.

When I asked Kava to describe the hardest part about running her one-year-old subscription business, I expected her to say that finding subscribers was the toughest challenge. In fact, the most difficult part of the business, she said, was working with her chocolate makers to fulfill large orders.

When you have thousands of subscribers, it can be difficult to find specialty chocolate makers willing to offer the bulk discount Kava needs for the Standard Cocoa business model to make sense. Specialty manufacturers of chocolate—or virtually any other craft product—by definition do not enjoy economies of scale. Just one order from Standard Cocoa could suck up manufacturing capacity for a craft chocolate maker for a month.

Kava tries to make the case that by being featured in a Standard Cocoa box, the company's chocolate is going to reach thousands of potential customers, representing a significant marketing opportunity for them. But that can be a difficult case to make to someone working from a facility that looks more like your mom's kitchen than a Lindt factory.

To make the surprise box model work, you need a large and varied network of manufacturers who are willing to give you a deep discount for a onetime order *and* who have the capacity to fulfill. Unlike Standard Cocoa, BarkBox offers unique products each month that are not necessarily craft or specialty, which leaves them open to placing an order with a large supplier that is able to fulfill a 200,000-unit purchase.

The Trojan Horse

According to Greek mythology, the city of Troy was fought over by the Greeks and the Trojans. Legend has it that after a ten-year stalemate, the Greeks came up with an ingenious plan. They built a large wooden horse and hid an elite fighting force inside. The Greeks then left town, giving the impression they had retreated. Assuming victory, the Trojans pulled the horse into the center of the walled city as a trophy of their victory. That night, the men hiding inside the horse crept out and opened the gates of the city to the rest of the Greek forces, which had returned under cover of night. The Greeks ambushed the sleeping Trojans and decisively took the city of Troy.

Many surprise box subscriptions are a Trojan horse. Companies give you various samples of products each month for a small price, but their bigger goal, disguised by the subscription, is actually to create a robust e-commerce site for their products.

Let's take a closer look at Conscious Box. For around $20 a month, you can subscribe to receive a sample box of all-natural, non-GMO products like snacks, cosmetics, and non-toxic cleaners. Ninety percent of Conscious Box customers are women, half are mothers, and all care deeply about discovering all-natural product alternatives.

Unlike BarkBox, which supplies subscribers with full-size packages of dog toys and treats, Conscious Box is focused on providing samples of products it gets free from the its suppliers (who typically have a sampling budget). If you discover something you like in your monthly Conscious Box, you are encouraged to rate the product on the Conscious Box website. You get 10 points per product rating, and for every 100 points you earn, you get a dollar to spend in the Conscious Box online store. Between 5% and 20% of Conscious Box subscribers rate a product in their box each month, developing a cache of valuable points to spend in the Conscious Box store.

Conscious Box doesn't give you a dollar off your next subscription for writing product reviews. The points go toward a purchase in the online store, because the company wants you to get in the habit of buying the full-size version of whatever you like from that monthly sampler box. The Conscious Box rating system is an elegant way to convert subscribers into online shoppers.

Conscious Box launched in 2012. Two years later, it was up to 30,000 subscribers. When I spoke with CEO Patrick Kelly, he told me Conscious Box's first goal was to build its subscriber base, but now that it has a large pool of subscribers, it is moving more aggressively into encouraging subscribers to buy full-size versions of the samples. As of April 2014, about 10% of Conscious Box revenue was coming from subscribers buying full-size versions of products at the Conscious Box online store.

The Blessing (and Curse) of Data

Data becomes both a blessing and a curse for companies like Conscious Box. Its sophisticated rating platform gives Conscious Box and its product suppliers tons of customer data. The challenge is that once customers take the time to tell you want they want, they expect you to use that information to improve the subscriber experience.

If you tell Conscious Box you're allergic to wheat, for example, then you damn well expect the company not to include a whole-wheat granola bar in your monthly box. To solve this challenge, Conscious Box offers three versions of its box: classic, gluten-free, and vegan. Reacting to all of that customer data creates a logistics and shipping challenge. It's one thing to know what your customer wants, but it's a bigger challenge to ensure you have just enough product to ship out in each box and on time.

That logistical challenge is one of the biggest reasons companies turn to e-commerce subscription platforms like Cratejoy, according to founder Amir Elaguizy. Cratejoy makes sure all your customer payments are collected on the same day so you know how much product to order from your suppliers. Cratejoy also gets you to lock in a cutoff date for when a subscriber can change her subscription, which relates to the ship date when the boxes leave your distribution center.

When you layer in customer preferences and their physical location, the shipping complexity of these businesses can become daunting—so you need to be comfortable with logistics, or partner with someone who is, in order to succeed.

WHO THE SURPRISE BOX MODEL WORKS BEST FOR

Consider the surprise box model if you have:

- A passionate, clearly defined market of consumers.

- A large and varied network of manufacturers that are willing to give you a deep discount for a onetime order and have the capacity to fulfill it.

- The ability to handle the logistics of shipping a physical product.

- A desire to use subscriptions to establish, Trojan Horse–style, a larger e-commerce site.

What the Insiders Say

- A big part of the reason people subscribe is the joy of finding something new. Consider how you'll keep surprising subscribers with new products, month after month.

- Don't underestimate the challenge of logistics and fulfillment. The more data you collect from your subscribers, the more they will expect you to customize their experience by sending them items based on their reported preferences. This increases the complexity of fulfillment exponentially.

CHAPTER 9

The Simplifier Model

Technology was supposed to simplify our lives—so why do I feel overwhelmed?

When I was a kid, we had a TV with a dial on it. I actually had to get off the couch to change the channel to one of the other 11. Before long we had the remote control—no more jumping off the couch, which was a good thing because the selection of channels had ballooned to more than 30.

These days we still have TV, but it's more complicated. There are hundreds of channels to choose from, plus we can watch shows and movies on NetFlix, Hulu, iTunes, etc. And that's just the content. The hardware is a spaghetti-ball collection of speakers, subwoofers, amplifiers, and the like. It's all a bit much.

Cars used to come with knobs; now they have onboard computers you need to master to do anything from turning on the air conditioner to unlocking the doors.

As kids, we used to play until the streetlights came on. Now our children have an endless parade of programs, lessons, and teams, each with its own set of rules, procedures, guidelines, and sign-off forms. Parents must now have a master's degree in logistics just to coordinate the orchestra of activity drop-offs and pick-ups.

In the old days, you showed up at the bank counter and the teller was the one who interfaced with the bank's systems. With online banking, we can avoid the trip to the teller, but it is yet another system to master.

System Overload

Taken separately, no one system is too complex for the average person to master. It is the *number* of systems we each must now use on a daily basis—combined with our generally overprogrammed lives—that causes our mental overload. When that happens, we want to outsource scheduling, planning, and time management to our technologies.

If you need more evidence, take a look at the meteoric rise of productivity applications designed to help keep us organized. The to-do list application called Any.do blossomed from 550,000 users in 2012 to 5 million users a year later. Wunderlist, another to-do list manager, grew from 1.5 million users in 2011 to 5.5 million users by the end of 2013.[1]

The big technology companies are starting to put serious money into helping people de-clutter and de-stress. In the fall of 2013, Apple bought Cue, a personal assistant application, for $40 million. Also in 2013, Dropbox paid $100 million for an inbox management application called Mailbox.

The hard drive in our collective brain is getting dangerously close to overload. This has given rise to the subscription model I call the simplifier. With the simplifier model, you offer to take one or more recurring tasks off your customers' to-do lists. Like all of the types of subscription businesses I'm presenting in this book, the simplifier model is not necessarily reserved for venture-funded tech start-ups. Virtually any company serving busy consumers can benefit from offering a simplifier subscription—and the richer your customers, the more acute their need for simplification.

Your House on Subscription

Take Frank Islam and his wife, Debbie Driesman. In 2007, Islam sold QSS Group for a reported $250 million.[2] Islam and Driesman took part of their windfall and built a 47,000-square-foot French château-inspired trophy house in Potomac, Maryland, complete with 14 bedrooms, 22 bathrooms, a movie theater, a gym, and some 60 chandeliers.[3]

That's a lot of lightbulbs to change, which is why Islam and Driesman subscribe to a program called Hassle Free Home Services, a classic simplifier subscription business that, for a fixed monthly fee, will manage the routine tasks that pile up on a home owner's to-do list.

Hassle Free Home Services prices subscriptions to its H.O.M.E. (Home Ownership Made Easy) program based on the size of your house; a standard four-bedroom home runs around $350 per month. Subscribers are assigned a technician who will manage their house throughout the year. Each month, your technician will run through a 100-point inspection to make sure everything from your smoke alarm batteries to your furnace filter are working properly. If something needs replacing, your technician handles it, and the replacement parts are all included in your $350 monthly nut.

Jim Vagonis started Washington, DC–area-based Hassle Free Home Services to help simplify home ownership. I asked Vagonis why customers subscribe to the H.O.M.E. program. "The owner wants to return from work, put their feet up, and simply enjoy their home without the hassles of a daily to-do list," he said.

For his part, Vagonis enjoys the predictability of the subscription business model. Typically, contractors lead a roller-coaster life defined by periods of 16-hour days followed by spells of underemployment. By contrast, Hassle Free Home Services has an annual contract renewal rate of more than 90%, so Vagonis can accurately forecast his labor needs and plan his business well into the future. "I can sit down in January and tell my guys how many hours I'll need them for in July," says Vagonis.

Up-selling and Cross-selling Subscribers

Like many subscription models, the frequency of customer contact inherent with monthly simplifier model subscriptions is great for up-selling and cross-selling subscribers. In the case of Hassle Free Home Services, your monthly onsite inspection is supplemented by helpful e-mail summaries, statements, and reminders of work that has been done and work that is planned. All told, Vagonis estimates he is in touch with his customers via one medium or another every week.

All of that interaction breeds familiarity over time, which means Hassle Free Home Services quickly becomes a trusted resource for all things related to the houses it manages. When big jobs that fall outside of the typical services covered under the 100-point monthly inspection come along, Vagonis often gets the call to come in and handle the job for an extra fee. Unlike a typical contractor who needs to submit an estimate alongside three other bidders, Vagonis is usually the only bidder because of the ongoing relationship he enjoys with the home owner.

Today, half of Hassle Free Home Services's revenue comes from general contracting work, and for most of those projects, Vagonis never had to enter a margin-grinding beauty contest to win.

Set It and Forget It

The simplifier model promises two things: not only will you take to-do items off your customer's list, you will also be the one reminding the customer that the task needs doing. One part of why we're feeling overwhelmed is the length of our to-do lists; the other part is trying to remember all of our tasks and commitments. Remembering takes up space on our mental hard drive, which leads to anxiety and a sense of being overwhelmed.

We met the Richmond, Virginia–based company Mosquito Squad in chapter 2. The company offers to keep bugs off your patio by spraying your backyard regularly with a proprietary chemical recipe approved by the Environmental Protection Agency.

You don't call Mosquito Squad when you need them; instead, Mosquito Squad operates on a subscription basis. Now you don't have to remember to buy citronella candles at the hardware store on the eve of a big backyard party. With Mosquito Squad's annual contract, your backyard living space will already be protected. Your life is made simpler, and so is that of the Mosquito Squad franchisees, who renew three quarters of annual spraying contracts each year.

A typical Mosquito Squad franchisee is an owner-operated company with annual revenue of less than $500,000. Very small personal-service businesses usually live a hand-to-mouth existence, always worrying where their revenue will come from next month. By contrast, the typical Mosquito Squad franchisee knows where 73% of next year's revenue will come from, through the automatic renewal of this year's contracts. This base of recurring revenue is a big reason these small companies pump out profit margins of 20% to 30% before tax.

The simplifier model works in many industries. The customer doesn't need to remember to call; instead, the savvy lawn-care company knows the customer's grass needs cutting once a week and sets up a recurring contract. Not only does your grass get cut; you no longer have to remember the task. Likewise, the smart swimming pool company doesn't wait for a customer to come into the store in a mad panic because his pool has turned green because he forgot to rebalance the chemicals. Instead, it will have set up an annual maintenance subscription for its customers, including pool opening, regular cleaning, and chemical balancing throughout the summer, in addition to closing the pool in the fall, all via an annual subscription.

There is enormous value in the "set it and forget it" value proposition. You get the recurring revenue and steady work, and your customer gets the benefit of knowing it's one less thing to remember to do.

WHO THE SIMPLIFIER MODEL WORKS BEST FOR

Consider the simplifier model if you have:

- A service that your customers need on an ongoing basis.

- The ability to sell to relatively affluent, busy consumers.

- A personal service business like pet grooming, massage, tutoring, window cleaning, carpet cleaning, bookkeeping, etc.

What the Insiders Say

- Discover your simplifier model by interviewing your target customer. Have her describe a typical day and ask her to show you her to-do list. Ask yourself what you could offer to tick something off that list.

- Part of the value proposition of the simplifier model is that you will remember to do a task so your customer doesn't have to. Therefore, make sure you set up a regular schedule for delivering your service. If you say you are going to be there the second Tuesday of every month, commit to it so the part of your customer's brain that wonders when you're coming next can turn off and relax.

- An ongoing service contract is a platform for cross-selling and upselling. Delivering the tasks associated with your service contract offers a built-in way to see what else you could provide your customer. You don't need to bundle all your services into a contract; just pick the ones a customer needs regularly, and those tasks should act as a platform to ensure you're the first person they think of for other jobs.

CHAPTER 10

The Network Model

One of the first subscription business models dates all the way back to January 28, 1878, in the town of New Haven, Connecticut.[1] A new device called a telephone had recently been invented, and 21 subscribers paid $1.50 per month to have access to a phone line. Three weeks later, there were 50 subscribers to the new service, and the first-ever telephone directory was published. Most of the listings were of doctors or town officials, such as the police and the post office. Eleven residences were listed, four of which were employees of the phone company.

It would have been impossible for one individual to build a telephone network to connect all of his relatives and friends. But if enough people in town chipped in a few dollars a month, the phone company had enough money to run the wires and build the network. Ever since then, companies have used the network model to provide partial access to expensive infrastructure.

One of the defining characteristics of the network model is that, unlike the private club model, the utility of the subscription increases as more people subscribe. If you lived in New Haven in February 1878, the only people you could call on a phone were a couple of doctors, the sheriff, and the post office. By the 1960s, virtually every house in New Haven had a phone and a listing in the directory, and the utility of being part of the network had grown exponentially.

User Marketing

One thing that makes the network model unique is that the users themselves have a vested interest in promoting the subscription because the more people who subscribe, the better it is for everyone.

For a dollar per year, subscribers to the messaging platform WhatsApp can send an unlimited number of messages to one another for free, because, instead of routing the messages through a mobile carrier's network, WhatsApp messages are sent via the Internet.

Once you've download the WhatsApp application on your mobile phone, you can send a free message to any other WhatsApp user. This tactic worked, and the user base grew exponentially. By early 2014, WhatsApp users were sharing more pictures than were posted on Facebook and the service had twice as many users as Twitter. WhatsApp was adding a million users *a day* when Facebook decided it had to buy them for $19 billion.

WhatsApp is a classic network model subscription, in which the value of being a subscriber increases as more people subscribe. What's more, your subscribers act as free marketers for your service. WhatsApp users save money on text-messaging fees, and they encourage their friends to sign on. At the time it was acquired, WhatsApp did not employ a single marketing executive.[2]

Driven by Density

Like WhatsApp, Zipcar has a base of passionate subscribers who actively promote the service to their friends. Zipcar's road to becoming a successful network model subscription company, however, was a little rockier.

The company was started in 1999 by Robin Chase and Antje Danielson. Danielson had returned from a trip to Berlin, where she had been impressed by a car-sharing scheme used in Germany and Switzerland. The partners decided to bring the model of sharing cars to North America.

The model was simple. You paid an annual membership fee of $50 a month, which granted you access to one of Zipcar's fleets. You were then charged for your part-time wheels by the hour or the day.

By June 2000, Chase and Danielson had raised $50,000 from an angel investor and leased their first 12 cars in Boston.[3] The partners quickly expanded and brought on more investors; by the end of 2002, Zipcar was up to 6,000 subscribers in Boston, New York City, and Washington, DC.

But not all was happy in Zipland. Zipcar was hemorrhaging cash. When Chase failed to deliver on an expected round of financing, the board replaced her as CEO with technology entrepreneur Scott Griffith.[4]

One of Griffith's first moves as CEO was to commission a series of focus groups among people who had considered using Zipcar but had chosen *not* to subscribe. The focus groups revealed that the main reason interested people didn't become subscribers was that they were worried about not being able to have access to a Zipcar when they wanted one.

At the time, Zipcar was spread too thin, with subscribers all over the cities it operated in. Griffith realized that, like any network model subscription, the value proposition of subscribing increased with the density of members. The more people who subscribed in an area, the more cars he could provide and the better it would be for everyone. But densely covering cities like Boston, Washington, and New York would be a daunting task; Griffiths figured he needed 150 to 200 cars per city. He also calculated that to be profitable, he needed a 40:1 ratio of members to cars. Since Zipcar was operating in three cities, he estimated it needed between 18,000 and 24,000 subscribers to become viable.

Instead of focusing on the big number of 18,000 to 24,000 members, Griffiths decided to break each city down into smaller zones and build density one zone at a time. For example, Zipcar divided Boston up into 12 geographic sections and then leveraged the demographics of each area to design its fleet. In Boston's well-to-do Beacon Hill neighborhood, Zipcar provided Volvos and BMWs.[5] In the left-leaning area of Cambridge, the fleet was made up mostly of Toyota's Prius hybrids.

Zipcar also matched the fleet in each zone with the usage pattern of subscribers in the area. Boston's Back Bay users often took their cars to Cape Cod for the weekend, so Zipcar made sure its vehicles were larger and more comfortable. Harvard Square subscribers were mostly students who wanted small cars for quick trips.

Once the fleet matched the demographics of a zone, Zipcar blitzed the neighborhood with advertising to sign up subscribers and build density. The immediate experience of users in the zone was positive, and they told their friends. Zipcar used this density model to scale up the company. Once it achieved success in its original founding markets, it was able to expand, which further increased the value proposition for Zipcar members.

Today, a Boston-based subscriber can not only find a car in her neighborhood, she can just as easily hop out of a train in Baltimore or a plane in Bristol, UK, and find a Zipcar.

Thanks to leveraging the network model, Griffiths had built the company up to more than $100 million in revenue and 760,000 subscribers when Avis Budget Group acquired it in 2013 for $491 million.[6]

The Network Effect in Reverse

The word-of-mouth advertising that helps you build a subscription business using the network model can also work in reverse.

Let's take a look at the dramatic rise and recent stumble of World of Warcraft, a fantasy adventure video game in the genre commonly referred to as MMORPGs (massively multiplayer online role-playing games). With a MMORPG, thousands of players in a game world interact with each other at the same time.

Much of the game's content is geared toward groups of players working together to explore a fantasy world of dangerous monsters and various evildoers. As with all network subscription models, the more people you know who are playing, the more fun for everyone.

World of Warcraft grew subscribers exponentially, from 1.5 million in 2005 to 12 million in 2010 before it started to stumble. Some subscribers perceived Warcraft to be losing its edge and not keeping up with competitive offerings from other games. They left in droves; between Q1 2012 and Q2 2012, World of Warcraft lost more than a million subscribers. The same users who encouraged their friends to join were now telling them to quit World of Warcraft and move to alternatives. By Q1 2014, World of Warcraft had finally stopped the bleeding and stabilized subscription levels by announcing new releases of the game, but the damage had been done. World of Warcraft is now down to around 7.6 million subscribers worldwide.[7]

If you're going to rely on an army of customer advocates to build your network model subscription business, make sure you have a listening mechanism in place so you can quickly react to subscriber dissatisfaction before the word of mouth that helped you build the network starts to act against you.

WHO THE NETWORK MODEL WORKS BEST FOR

Consider the network model if you have:

- A product or service whose utility improves as increasing numbers of people join in.

- The network model works best when you offer a remarkable experience people feel compelled to share. If your product is only, say, 5% better than the alternative, this is likely not the best model for you.

- Tech-savvy customers and prospects. The more socially connected your customers, the faster your network business will grow.

What the Insiders Say

- You need subscribers to build the network, but you need a network to attract subscribers. Focus your limited resources on a small, tightly defined group of early-adopting customers. Build density before moving to your next market.

- The network model is best for companies that have a lot of capital or entrepreneurs who are good at raising it. In the case of Zipcar's first decade, the business was always hungry for cash. To begin, Chase and Danielson started off with an angel investment, then raised $4.7 million in a second round of financing two years later. With Griffiths in the driver's seat, Zipcar raised $25 million in 2006 and another $21 million in 2010.[8] At WhatsApp, founders Jan Koum and Brian Acton started out with a $250,000 seed round of financing in 2009, then raised another $8 million in 2011 and another $50 million in the summer of 2013.[9]

- The good news is that once you build the network, the cost to enter the market, coupled with a network of happy users who benefit from promoting you, becomes a protective shield against would-be competitors. The word of mouth from your passionate user base helps guide and fuel your growth by providing free market research about the new products, features, and benefits they want you to offer next.

- The bad news is that if subscribers flip from happy to dissatisfied, the same powerful force that helps you grow a network model subscription business can start to work against you.

CHAPTER 11

The Peace-of-Mind Model

People with dogs are always worried about losing them. One whiff of a skunk and the family dog can be halfway down the block before you even know he's gone.

That's where Tagg comes in. Tagg is a pet-tracking service started by Snaptracs, a subsidiary of wireless giant Qualcomm that had 30,000 subscribers by the summer of 2013.[1] With Tagg, you can keep an eye on Rover with your mobile phone. First, you buy the collar from a retailer like Verizon Wireless or Best Buy. Then you set up the monitoring service for $7.95 per month. If your dog leaves a specified area (that you determine), you get an alert on your smartphone.

Tagg is an example of what I call the peace-of-mind model, which offers insurance against something your customers hope they'll never need. You are there to help your customers when they need your service, but otherwise you stay out of their way. You make money from charging more in subscription revenue than it costs you to deliver the service when called upon. You can also jack up your profits by investing the money your customers give you before they need your service.

Would It Work in Your Industry?

If you sell something people care about, you can consider the peace-of-mind model for your subscription business.

When you sign on with a home security company like ADT, you pay a few dollars a month in return for the peace of mind that comes from knowing that if you ever need them, the company will be there.

If you want to monitor the whereabouts of your car and be notified of its location in the event of theft, you can subscribe to the LoJack Stolen Vehicle Recovery System.

People also care about their laptops, so for $39.99 a year, LoJack will keep an eye on your MacBook if you subscribe to its LoJack for Laptops service. Through its partnership with Absolute Software, Lo-Jack will track your laptop so you can always pinpoint where it is.

LoJack has gone well beyond selling monitoring for products and now sells monitoring for people too. If your dad suffers from Alzheimer's, for $30 a month you can hook him up to SafetyNet by LoJack, which will track his location through a GPS-enabled wristband if he goes missing.

One of the challenges of the peace-of-mind model is guessing how frequently your customers will need your service. Underestimate and you will end up spending more than you collect in premiums. Overestimate significantly and you will be susceptible to competitors offering to insure your customers at a lower rate or having your customers opt to "self-insure," which means they opt to bypass insurance altogether.

A little history can help guide you in setting your price. If you look back over the course of a year, how many times does a typical customer call you, and what does that service call cost you to deliver? Provided you charge more in premiums than you expect to pay out in services provided, you will earn an *underwriting profit*—the amount of money you earn for taking the risk that, if the customer calls more frequently than you expected, you still need to honor your end of the bargain.

Businesses Also Buy Peace of Mind

It's not just consumers who buy peace of mind. Businesses also buy monitoring and insurance protection they hope they will never need.

Website monitoring companies like Site24x7.com will keep an eye on your website to ensure it doesn't go down. If there is a problem, you're notified immediately.

In the event someone starts bad-mouthing your company on Twitter, the Radian6 team will give you a heads up. Radian6 pioneered the "online reputation monitoring and management" industry before it was acquired by fellow subscription business Salesforce.com in 2011.[2] Companies like Honda and Cisco use Radian6 to listen to the conversation about their brands on social networks so they can know what people are saying about them and tell their side of a story when bad buzz happens online.

Like all insurance, the peace-of-mind model for subscriptions is selling the serenity of knowing that, in the event of a catastrophe, you're covered. This can work when you're selling to both consumers and businesses, but to apply it in your industry, it's helpful to understand how insurance companies make money.

The Magic of Float

Most people think insurers profit simply by charging more for premiums than they actually pay out in claims. While this underwriting profit is important, the real money is made from something called float.

Underwriting profit is the difference between premiums generated and claims paid, while *float* is the money you make investing the cash people pay in insurance premiums before they make a claim.

Warren Buffett described how he uses float in his 2009 letter to Berkshire Hathaway shareholders:

> **Our float has grown from $16 million in 1967, when we entered the business, to $62 billion at the end of 2009. Moreover, we have now operated at an underwriting profit for seven consecutive years. I believe it likely that we will continue to underwrite profitably in most—though certainly not all—future years. If we do so, our float will be cost-free, much as if someone deposited $62 billion with us that we could invest for our own benefit without the payment of interest.[3]**

Sound a little too complicated for your business? It doesn't have to be. Let's imagine you install roofs and decide to offer a peace-of-mind subscription service. For $20 a month, you offer your customers the guarantee that, should their roof get damaged or need repair, you will return to fix it at your cost.

After a year, assuming the customer has not called, you've collected $240 ($20 x 12). You could keep the $240 in your pocket or invest it. Big insurance companies would invest this "float" in the stock market, but you might decide to invest the $240 back into your business and buy a new sign for your van.

Let's imagine the same scenario plays out for four more years: you collect $240 each year and invest it in your business and your customer never made a claim. Now you've collected a total of $1,200. In the sixth year, your customer calls and asks you to come and repair his roof, which has been damaged in a storm. It costs you $800 to make the repair.

The customer is happy because he just got his roof repaired without paying for a service call. You're satisfied because you've earned an underwriting profit of $400 ($1,200–$800). But your true return is much greater because you have had $1,200 of your customer's money—interest free—to invest in your business. You have taken on a risk in guaranteeing your customer's roof replacement and need to be paid for placing that bet. The repair job could have cost you $3,000, and then you would have taken an underwriting loss of $1,800 ($1,200–$3,000).

Calculating your risk is the primary challenge of running a peace-of-mind model company. Big insurance companies employ an army of actuaries who use statistical models to predict the likelihood of a claim being made. You don't need to be quite so scientific. Instead, start by looking back at the last 20 roofs you've installed with a guarantee and figure out how many service calls you needed to make. That will give you a pretty good idea of the possible risk of offering a peace-of-mind subscription.

Assuming you're not an actuary and you didn't get your doctorate in math from MIT, it's probably a wise idea to go slow in leveraging the peace-of-mind subscription model. You can limit your risk in a number of ways:

- Offer the peace-of-mind subscription only to a handful of customers so you can get a sense of how often claims are made.
- Limit your customer offer. A roofer could offer to cover repairs *up to* a certain dollar amount or for damage caused for a limited number of reasons.
- Reinsure the risk by buying an insurance policy of your own that covers you for an unexpected volume of claims.

WHO THE PEACE-OF-MIND MODEL WORKS BEST FOR

Consider the peace-of-mind model if you have:

- Something that is difficult, expensive, or impossible to replace.

- A business that allows you to absorb the cost of a claim by leveraging your existing assets rather than paying out cash. In the roofing example, you already have the crew, ladders, and trucks for installing roofs, so your cost to honor a claim may be minimal.

- A history of customer service calls that helps you predict the likelihood and frequency of claims.

What the Insiders Say

- Limit your risk. Premiums may look like free money, but you need to ensure you have the resources and infrastructure to honor your commitment in case your customer calls.

- The peace-of-mind model is different than the simplifier model, in which you set up a service contract to preemptively service your customers. In the peace-of-mind model, you're offering an insurance to help only *if* your customer needs it.

Using the Nine Subscription Models in Your Own Business

My list of nine subscription models is definitely incomplete. You could argue that there are entire models I've missed or companies I've omitted that deserve to be mentioned as examples. Also, as time goes on, I'm sure we'll see new models emerge that haven't yet been contemplated.

My hope, however, is that by seeing the range of subscription models that are out there, you'll be able to jot down a few possibilities for launching your own subscription business or complementing your existing business with some recurring revenue. I hope you agree that while cloud-based software companies and media titans have pioneered the subscription business, it is a model that you too can leverage, whether you own a law practice, a coffee shop, or a day-care center.

Next, let's dig into the hard work of actually building a subscription business.

PART THREE

Building Your Subscription Business

Many traditional businesses become successful based on the sheer force of the owner's personality. When sales are down, the owner leverages his network and brings in business. When a customer is unhappy, it is the owner who uses her diplomacy to smooth things over. But in a subscription business, the very structure and nature of the business usually means you will go relatively quickly from handling a few customers at a time to juggling a larger group of subscribers.

I've started a few businesses in my life. I've had a radio production business, a design agency, an events company, a quantitative research business, and a software company. I'm involved in my second subscription business, and while subscription businesses are in many ways more rewarding than the others, they are also more challenging in many respects.

Metaphorically speaking, a traditional business requires more brawn, while a subscription business requires more brain.

In a subscription business, any decision you make affects your entire base of subscribers all at once. Sending a single e-mail can trigger an avalanche of cancellations. Rather than collecting a few invoices, you have to figure out how to charge potentially thousands of credit cards a month, each with its own expiration date and credit limit. While gathering more customer data is great, your subscription business may collect so much data that you have to figure out which bits of information are critical and which are just noise. It's a ball of complexity that will challenge you intellectually.

This last section of this book is designed to help you find shortcuts through some of the hardest lessons that I and many of the subscription business operators I interviewed have learned about setting up and building a subscription-based revenue stream.

CHAPTER 12

The New Math

One of the most challenging aspects of building a subscription business is the need to relearn the basics of how you measure your progress.

Traditionally, you have probably measured your business using a profit-and-loss (P&L) statement, which counts the amount of money you make after you pay your expenses and the cost to make whatever it is you sell.

In a subscription business, instead of selling a finite offering, you are essentially renting access to your product or service over time. This means your accountant will spread the revenue you get from a subscription over the life of the agreement between you and your customer. The moment you switch to a subscription model your P&L will start to look ugly.

Let's take a look at how the P&L of a typical software company changes after it transforms from a traditional business to a subscription business. In the old model, a software company would sell the customer the product outright. Customers would receive a physical box and a few installation CDs that they would get to keep forever. After the customer paid, say, $1,000 for the software, the company that sold it would have $1,000 show up in the revenue line of its P&L for the month in which it made the sale.

In moving to a subscription model, the company allows the customers to rent the software instead of purchasing it. Let's imagine the same software costs $99 per month to rent. Now when the company makes a sale, instead of $1,000 showing up on its revenue line, it gets to account for only $99 in the month in which it makes the sale—just one tenth of what it would have seen on its P&L using the old model.

Of course, the economic benefit of having $99 a month over a period of years far outweighs the one-time bump of $1,000, but psychologically the switch to a subscription model can be paralyzing for a company or owner who is used to seeing black at the bottom of the P&L each month.

This phenomenon of applying old measuring sticks to a new game was a contributing factor to the failure of my first attempt at shifting my consulting company to a subscription model. We had built a successful project-based consultancy serving blue-chip clients like Bank of America, IBM, and Wells Fargo. A typical project would generate $50,000 in consulting fees over a period of a couple of months. Therefore, on our P&L statement, a $50,000 project would show up in two $25,000 installments spread across the two months in which we did the work. In a typical month, we would show a profit of somewhere between 20% and 30% before tax.

Sick and tired of the hamster wheel that is the sell/do approach to business, we switched to a subscription model. Instead of doing "one-shot" consulting, we decided to offer our advice and research on subscription for an annual fee of around $30,000. As we shifted our business model, our P&L went from looking healthy to looking horrible. According to Generally Accepted Accounting Principles (GAAP), a subscription is recognized on the P&L in equal installments over the life of the subscription. So instead of seeing $25,000 in revenue from a client in the months in which we made the sale and did the work, we were showing $2,500 of a client's $30,000-per-year subscription each month.

Overnight, we went from making money on paper to losing gobs of it. I rationalized one month of losses to myself, saying it was normal to have a short period of losses as we switched business models. After the second month of losses, my accountant started asking questions about what we had changed and why we were so focused on what was obviously a losing strategy. By the third month of losses, I was in full panic mode. No matter how many subscriptions we sold, we still showed losses on the P&L.

By the fourth month, we returned to offering project-based consulting so that our P&L would start looking healthy again. For a few months we ran the models in parallel, offering both custom consulting and a subscription. Knowing they could buy our services on a one-shot basis, our customers cooled to the subscription model, and we ended up shutting down the subscription altogether. It felt good to see the numbers turn from red to black on our P&L. Little did I know; what felt good was also dead wrong.

What I didn't realize at the time was that by shutting down the subscription business, we were retreating from a strategy that could have transformed us into a valuable company. Unlike a sell/do consultancy, which is virtually worthless to a buyer, we had been building recurring revenue. What's more, since we charged up front for our $30,000 subscription, our cash flow was fine. I just couldn't get the losses on the P&L out of my head. We had taken a giant step backward in terms of our progress as a company, all because I was looking at the wrong numbers.

The New Measuring Sticks

In a subscription business, understanding your financial performance requires a new set of operating statistics. The foundation of your subscription business is built on your *monthly recurring revenue* (MRR). This is the recurring revenue listed on your company's P&L every month. When a customer subscribes to a membership website for $99 per year, the company gets to recognize that revenue on its P&L at the MRR rate of $8.25 ($99 divided by 12).

The next number you need to understand is the *lifetime value* (LTV) of a subscriber. LTV is calculated by multiplying your MRR by the number of months your customer stays with you, less the cost of serving them during the life of the subscription. To keep things simple, let's imagine you don't have client managers serving subscribers, so we'll assume the cost to service subscribers is zero. If your average subscriber stays with you for 30 months, then the LTV of a subscriber is 30 x $8.25 = $247.50.

The next data point you need to assess the health of your subscription business is your *customer acquisition cost* (CAC). This is the amount of money you spend on sales and marketing to win a new subscriber. If your company's total expenditure on sales and marketing last month was $2,000 and you acquired 25 subscribers, your CAC would be $80 during that period ($2,000 divided by 25).

Your true CAC will be revealed after you pick the low-hanging fruit. Your friends, family, and best customers will likely subscribe to your new offering out of loyalty to you and a desire to encourage your new business, so you need to discount these early subscribers in your calculation. To truly understand your CAC, you want to know what your CAC is at scale, meaning what is sustainable after the "love and guilt" subscriptions have been signed up.

The Viability Threshold

Once you know how much a subscriber is worth to you, and how much it costs to acquire one, you can start to estimate the viability and performance of your subscription business. This is something David Skok does all day long.

Skok is a general partner at the venture-capital firm Matrix Partners, where he evaluates potential investments in subscription businesses and advises the management team of his portfolio on existing investments; he works with companies such as HubSpot.com, Digium, CloudBees, Enservio, GrabCAD, OpenSpan, SageCloud, Salsify, and VideoIQ.

Not only does he invest in entrepreneurs, he is also one himself, having started four technology companies—three of which he took public on the NASDAQ exchange. Skok also writes *For Entrepreneurs*, a popular blog for technology entrepreneurs. It was there that he first published his most important metric for evaluating the performance of a subscription business:

LTV > 3 × CAC

Based on his experience running companies, and after evaluating hundreds of others for his venture fund, Skok has found that in order to be a viable subscription business over the long term, a company needs to have an LTV:CAC ratio of at least 3:1. He has seen some of the most successful subscription businesses achieve an LTV:CAC ratio as high as 8:1.

To return to our hypothetical example of a membership website with an LTV of $247.50 and a CAC of $80, it has achieved an LTV:CAC ratio of just over 3:1 ($247.50 divided by 80). Per Skok's estimation, this is a viable business model.

There may be many reasons to build subscriptions into your business. You may offer a subscription as a loss leader just to build a relationship with a customer who will buy more from you because he is a subscriber. You may also be able to monetize your subscribers through advertising or build a subscription offering just to collect data about your customer preferences. But if your goal is to build a stand-alone, scalable subscription company, focus on getting the LTV of a subscriber to be at least three times what it costs you to acquire her. Only then will you know it is time to hit the gas.

Churn

Arguably the most important factor contributing to the viability of your subscription business is the rate at which customers quit subscribing; this is known as your *churn rate*. To calculate your MRR churn rate, take your MRR at the beginning of the month and divide it by the amount of lost MRR in the month.

Let's say you have 1,000 subscribers who pay you $500 per month. Further, let's imagine a month when 18 of your customers leave. Your MRR is $500,000 ($500 x 1,000), and your lost MRR is 18 x $500 = $9,000, so your churn rate for the month is 1.8% ($9,000 divided by $500,000).

You can also calculate your monthly customer churn rate by taking the number of customers who leave you in a given month and dividing it by the total number of customers you had going into the month.

It's tempting to want a benchmark for what is acceptable churn, but the reality is that it varies dramatically according to the kind of subscription business you're in. If your product or service is a luxury people can do without, your monthly churn is likely going to be much higher than if you run a cloud-based software business selling crucial accounting software to large enterprise customers.

Most important, churn viewed in isolation is not as meaningful as looking at churn *in relation to how much it costs you to win new customers*. Using Skok's formula, you need to get your churn down to a point where, over the life of her subscription, your average customer is worth at least three times what it costs you to acquire her.

Margin

The other number you need to consider is the cost of serving each new subscriber. Considered part of your cost of goods sold, this number varies based on how many customers you bring on. For most subscription businesses, it includes the salary and other costs of the people you hire to get new customers onboard and serve them over time.

HubSpot.com is a software platform used to manage inbound

marketing. It allows a user to build a website, set up a blog, manage social media accounts, create e-mail marketing campaigns, and analyze it all through a dashboard. It's kind of like an all-in-one marketing platform for businesses. The typical HubSpot customer is a small to mid-size company that needs to present a professional online image but doesn't have the budget or internal resources to hire a team of designers.

When we signed up for HubSpot at SellabilityScore.com, there was a lot of work to do. We had to import all of our logos and images to the site, pick a standard font, and create a variety of template pages. It took a few weeks and probably 20 or 30 calls to HubSpot support to get it done. We were also assigned a consultant to help us get started and an account manager to go to with questions. This process is called *onboarding*, and getting it right can have a big effect on reducing the churn rate of your customers, which is why companies like HubSpot invest handsomely in onboarding.

HubSpot considers its support department and consultants as part of its cost of goods sold (COGS); in total, this cost makes up around 17% of MRR.[1] So for every $100 of MRR they have, they get $83 of gross profit after paying for the costs of onboarding its new customers.

How the Numbers Add Up

To see this alphabet soup of acronyms and calculations work together, we can look in more detail at the case of HubSpot. Back in Q1 2011, its numbers looked like this:

HUBSPOT	Q1 2011
Customer Acquisition Cost (CAC)	$6,025
Average MRR per customer	$429
Monthly MRR Churn Rate	3.5%
Margin	83%
LTV	$10,074

To begin to calculate its LTV:CAC, you take MRR x margin and divide it by the churn rate. Here's the math:

$429 x 83% (0.83) = $356.07 divided by 3.5% (0.035) = $10,074

Back in Q1 2011, HubSpot was in trouble. Its LTV:CAC ratio was a low 1.67 ($10,074 divided by $6,025).

When you look below the surface, HubSpot faced many challenges. Because of the complexity of what it sells, HubSpot can't rely on a website to sign people up. It needs salespeople to work the phones and explain the HubSpot value proposition. Since salespeople are expensive, its CAC is relatively high. It was also losing 3.5% of MRR per month, which amounts to almost half its revenue each year.

Throughout 2011, the HubSpot team worked hard on every facet of its business, from getting more efficient at acquiring new customers and onboarding them, to focusing on finding slightly larger businesses to sell to. By the first quarter of 2012, they had turned things around and had crested Skok's holy grail of a 3:1 LTV:CAC ratio.

HUBSPOT	Q1 2012
Customer Acquisition Cost (CAC)	$6,880
Average MRR per customer	$583
Monthly MRR Churn Rate	2.0%
Margin	81%
LTV	$23,775
LTV: CAC	3.5

What changed in a year to move HubSpot from an unsustainable subscription business to a viable one? At first glance, its Q1 2012 results look pretty similar, with the gross margin percentage still running in the low eighties. Its CAC was still north of $6,000 in Q1 2012—even a touch *higher*. But along with a slightly higher CAC, it had a 36% higher MRR. And the most dramatic improvement was the churn rate, which was cut almost in half, from 3.5% down to 2%, through better onboarding of new customers and targeting of larger businesses, among other tactics we'll talk about in the section on lowering churn in chapter 15.

Matching Your Sales Channel to the Complexity of Your Offer

One of the big decisions you need to make in implementing a subscription model is how you plan to win new subscribers. The more complex your offer, the more you will need to rely on humans to sell it.

What follows is a list of sales approaches often used by subscription businesses, ranked from most expensive to least:

1. *Field salespeople:* These are the people who visit customers face-to-face. For example, take Workday, which offers software that allows big companies to integrate their finance and HR functions. Given its complexity and long sales cycles, Workday salespeople often visit their customers in person and suffer through sales cycles that stretch over quarters or years.

2. *Telesales:* Salespeople who contact customers remotely—via telephone and e-mail—work over shorter sales cycles. HubSpot sells a relatively complex inbound marketing platform predominantly to small and mid-size companies through a telesales team whose typical sales cycle is weeks or months.

3. *Self-serve:* Subscribers don't need direct salesperson access in this system. Ancestry.com sells access to its archives and a simple family tree software package without employing outbound salespeople; instead, it relies on marketing copy and videos to explain the offering.

Let's take a look at how using the lowest-cost self-serve sales channel affects the overall economics of a business. Ancestry.com became a private company in 2013, but back in 2012, when it was a public company, it was still required to release its financials, which gives us the opportunity to crunch its numbers.

In Q2 2012, the average Ancestry.com customer generated $18.84 in MRR—just one-thirtieth the MRR of a HubSpot customer around the same time.[2] But unlike HubSpot, which uses a relatively expensive team of telephone salespeople to sell a complex product, Ancestry.com used simple videos to explain its offering. It offered users an elegant

14-day free-trial offer that automatically converted into a paying subscription on the 15th day.

By Q2 2012, Ancestry.com had gotten so good at acquiring self-serve customers that its CAC was down to $81.49. Even though Ancestry.com had a relatively high monthly churn rate of 3.4%, its efficiency at acquiring customers bailed them out, and its LTV:CAC ratio was a healthy 5.6. Here are the numbers:

ANCESTRY.COM	Q2 2012
Customer acquisition cost (CAC)	$81.49
Average MRR per customer	$18.84
Monthly MRR Churn Rate	3.4%
Margin	82.3%
LTV	$456
LTV: CAC	5.6

Experiment Offline

One of HubSpot's indirect competitors is a company called Constant Contact. It offers small businesses a platform to keep in touch with its customers through e-mail marketing and social media.

Constant Contact has been trying to optimize its metrics since its start in 1995. In January 2014, the company announced that its revenue was up to $285.4 million per year. It went from $100,000 MRR in 2002 to almost $24 million in MRR in 2014, but it has been what CEO Gail Goodman calls a "long, slow SaaS [software as a service] ramp of death." Far from an overnight success, Constant Contact has been tweaking its approach to optimize its numbers for almost two decades.

It has tried virtually every marketing tactic there is, from TV and radio advertising to search engine optimization (SEO), direct mail, and sending salespeople out into a community to cold-call by knocking on doors.

Constant Contact has tried hundreds of campaigns over the years, and one of the most successful had nothing at all to do with the Internet. Instead of doing all of its marketing online, the company hosts small, free offline workshops to teach business owners how to market their companies. To scale the approach, Constant Contact hired a group of 22 regional development directors, who each owned a physical territory. These directors approached local trade and business associations about hosting a seminar for their members.

After a ramp-up period, a typical regional development director hosts between two and four events per week. Each seminar usually draws 40 to 60 people and a percentage of them become Constant Contact subscribers. In 2012, this team of regional development directors taught 125,000 small businesses. The offline seminar approach has now become one of the key ways Constant Contact acquires new subscribers. Perhaps counterintuitively for a business that specializes in e-marketing connections, it got its CAC down to $450 by going offline and speaking with its subscribers in person.

Here are the Constant Contact numbers from 2012.[3]

CONSTANT CONTACT	2012
Customer acquisition cost (CAC)	$450
Average MRR per customer	$39
Monthly MRR Churn Rate	2.2%
Margin	72%
LTV	$1,276.36
LTV: CAC	2.8

Mosquito Squad still uses direct mail as a way to acquire customers. In a direct-mail campaign it launched in 2013, the company was able to get its CAC down to around $93. Given the typical operating metrics of a Mosquito Squad franchise, having a CAC as low as $93 gives it a whopping 13:1 LTV:CAC ratio.

MOSQUITO SQUAD	2013
Customer acquisition cost (CAC)	$93
Average MRR per customer	$50
Monthly MRR Churn Rate	2.3%
Margin	58%
LTV	$1,261
LTV: CAC	13.5

As you build your subscription business, you'll need to go beyond the P&L statement and develop a new set of measuring sticks to track your progress. Your LTV:CAC ratio is the hardest working statistic of the bunch because it is derived from all the key numbers you'll want to track. If you can get your LTV:CAC above 3:1, you may want to step on the gas. If you're below 3:1, it may be time to slow down and tinker with your model until you can crest the 3:1 milestone.

Either way, there is one more essential ingredient you'll need in order to build a subscription business. Cash is to a subscription business as oxygen is to humans. If you don't have it, no matter how healthy you are on other measures, you're dead. In the next chapter, we'll discuss how to find the money to grow your subscription business.

CHAPTER 13

The Cash Suck vs. the Cash Spigot

Understanding your LTV:CAC ratio helps you understand the theoretical long-term viability of your subscription business. There is a big difference, however, between viability on paper and viability in the real world, and the difference is a little something called cash.

If you go from charging $1,000 for your product to renting access to it for $99 a month, you may have a fatter LTV over time, but in the short run, you're going to have a lot less cash to work with. In fact, it will take you 10 long months to get the $1,000 in cash you would have received in one lump sum by selling it the old way.

In a subscription business, you receive your cash over time. In almost all cases, your MRR will be less than the cost to acquire a customer, which means it will take you a number of months to gain back the cash you spent to win that customer. The more aggressively you grow, the more of your cash gets sucked up in acquiring customers, which is why the number of months it takes you to recover the costs of winning a subscriber matters.

CAC Payback Period

Bessemer Venture Partners (BVP), a venture-capital firm that focuses on subscription-based software companies, has invested in such winners as LinkedIn, DocuSign, and LifeLock. BVP uses a concept called the CAC payback period as a way to evaluate investment opportunities and the performances of its portfolio companies. In layman's terms, the CAC payback period measures how many months it takes you to make back the cost of acquiring a customer.

$$\text{CAC Payback Period} = \frac{\text{Total Sales and Marketing Costs for the Month}}{\text{New MRR added for the Month}}$$

To use a simple example, let's say that in one month you acquired one customer who paid you $100 per month. If it cost you $500 in sales and marketing expenses to win that $100 in MRR, then you would have a CAC payback period of 5 months (500 divided by 100).

BVP, along with most professional investors, adds a twist that takes into consideration the gross margin of your subscription. Let's say you make 70% gross profit after paying the expenses of onboarding and any hard costs associated with adding each new subscriber.

$$\text{CAC Payback Period} = \frac{\text{Total Sales and Marketing Costs for the Month}}{\text{New MRR added} \times \text{Gross Margin}}$$

Using the example above, BVP would express your CAC payback period as approximately 7 months: 500 divided by ($100 x .70).

An acceptable CAC payback period depends on how sticky your customers are and how much they spend with you. BVP elaborates on this concept in its white paper "Bessemer's Top 10 Laws of Cloud Computing":

> **For SMB (Small & Medium Business) customers with higher churn rates and thus shorter monetization windows, CAC Payback Periods of 6–18 months are typically needed, whereas enterprise businesses with high up sells and long retention periods may be able to subsidize payback periods of 24–36 months. A CAC Payback Period of 36+ months is typically a cause for concern and suggests you may want to slam on the brakes until you can improve sales efficiency, whereas a Payback Period of under 6 months means you should invest more money immediately and step on the gas.[1]**

The concept of a CAC payback period can be described visually. Gordon Daugherty, as chief operating officer at Nimsoft, a company that CA Technologies acquired for $350 million back in 2010, created such a visual. Daugherty, now a partner and angel investor at Austin-based Capital Factory, was looking for a simple way to describe Nimsoft's key operating metrics to the rank-and-file employees of Nimsoft and its new parent, CA Technologies. The CAC payback graphic looked like this:

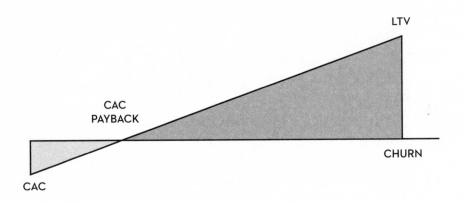

The X-axis of the graph is time (usually expressed in months); the Y-axis represents gross profit.

To go back to our earlier example, if your cost to acquire a customer is $500 and you earn $70 of gross profit per customer, then you're underwater by $430 in month one ($500–$70). In month two, you're getting closer to the CAC payback period because you now have a second month's worth of MRR. By month seven, you hit your CAC payback ($500 divided by $70). In month eight, you're in the area to the right of the CAC Payback intersection on the chart and are set to keep accumulating profit until the customer cancels the subscription.

The chart on the next page shows that when you have an expensive CAC, represented by the lower of the two dotted lines, your time to reach CAC payback lengthens and, assuming you control for churn, your LTV lowers. Likewise, as you get more efficient at acquiring customers, you break even sooner and enjoy more LTV, as expressed by the higher dotted line:

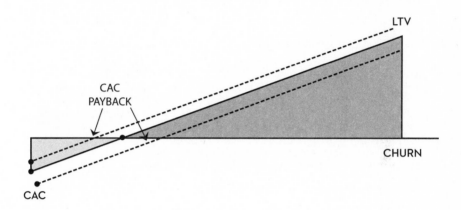

Three Choices to Fund Your Growth

Since your MRR per customer is almost certain to be a lot less than your CAC, you're going to need cash to grow your subscription business. Most successful subscription businesses also need to invest heavily in systems and branding up front, which is why a lot of them go outside to raise capital. In my experience, you have three fundamental choices to find the cash to grow your subscription business.

Cash Source 1: Rob Peter to Pay Paul

You can use cash from nonrecurring sources of your business to build your subscription offering. With this model, you take the profits from your traditional business, and instead of putting them in your pocket, you reinvest them into building your subscription offering.

Pursuing this strategy usually takes longer than raising a seven-figure seed round of outside money, but you get to keep control of your product and take your time building it.

Jason Fried and David Heinemeier Hansson used this cash-flow strategy to build their company, 37signals, which was renamed Basecamp in 2014. Basecamp started out as a project-based web-design company building sites for big companies and has evolved into one of the leading project-management software platforms available for small and mid-size companies. They used the cash from big, profitable, one-shot website projects to fund the development of Basecamp, which they sell for around $20 per month, per user. After a year of running the web-design shop in parallel with the subscription business, Basecamp had built up enough recurring revenue from subscribers to start saying no to new web-design projects. Today, it's entirely subscription-based.

FreshBooks.com used this same strategy to become the number-one subscription-based cloud accounting solution designed for small business owners in North America. It has now been used by more than 5 million people.

Mike McDerment developed the first generation of FreshBooks.com while running a four-person design studio. He was using Microsoft Word to send an invoice and hit Save instead of Save As, accidentally erasing an old invoice. With the old invoice gone, he had no way of tracking it for his business or the tax man. Determined to develop an invoicing tool that was easy to use for a small company like his, he developed FreshBooks.com as a side project.

"It took over sixteen months to bring a product to market," McDerment told me. "When we launched, no one cared, and twenty-four months after starting, we had only ten paying customers and revenues of $99 per month. We moved into my parents' basement for three and a half years."[2]

By 2014, FreshBooks had paying customers in 120 countries, and McDerment & Co. had moved out of his parent's basement into digs that housed more than 100 FreshBooks.com employees. And he did it without raising venture capital. FreshBooks was developed by using the money McDerment made from design jobs for one-shot customers.

It's true that this "rob Peter to pay Paul" strategy for funding your development may appear to contradict the sales strategy of giving your customer an "ultimatum" to subscribe or stop doing business. However, neither Basecamp nor FreshBooks were asking the same customers to subscribe or do one-shot projects. They were using cash from big customers to fund the development of a product that would end up being used mostly by very small customers. Their large customers would be unlikely to want to buy their product for smaller businesses, but that was okay, as the big guys had provided the cash to fund the development of the product for the small guys.

This bootstrapping approach to building your subscription business allows you to keep all (or most) of the equity in your company. Basecamp has shunned venture-capital investors and used the money from ongoing operations, and a minority investment from Amazon's Jeff Bezos, to fund its growth. The last time I spoke with Basecamp's Fried, in May 2014, the company had 43 employees, and Fried was focused on building an enduring business—not necessarily a big one. Fried had just made the decisions to change the company name from 37signals to Basecamp and to focus on its winning project-management software at the expense of its other products, such as Highrise, Campfire, and Backpack. If Basecamp had been a venture-capital-backed company, I doubt the backers would have allowed Fried to sunset the other components of his product suite—and the revenue opportunity they represented—in favor of just a single offering.

The downside of "rob Peter to pay Paul" is that it takes a lot longer to scale up. It took Fried a year of selling Basecamp before he had enough cash from subscribers to start saying no to web-design projects. At FreshBooks, it took McDerment two years to get 10 paying customers. Therefore, if you think you're competing in a winner-take-all category, where time to market is the key determinant of success,* then "rob Peter to pay Paul" may not be your best choice for funding your subscription business.

Cash Source 2: Outside Money

Your second option when building your subscription business is to go outside for capital. If you can prove your LTV:CAC ratio is north of 3:1 at scale, and your market is large enough, you'll probably have a line of investors willing to give you money to fund your subscription business. Here you're giving up equity, and usually some control, in return for the cash to build your subscription business.

Outside investors can bring a fresh perspective to your company, along with wisdom and hard-fought experiences, which they'll likely

---

* The "first mover advantage" concept is severely overhyped. Before there was FreshBooks, there was QuickBooks, before we had Basecamp we had Microsoft Project, and before Facebook there was Myspace. Most winning companies take a proven model and make it better, so you may want to ask yourself some hard questions before using "first mover advantage" as your justification for seeking outside capital.

be eager to share. But outside funds, especially venture capital, can be very expensive money.

Consider the story of Bloodhound Technologies. Joseph A. Carsanaro started Bloodhound back in the mid-1990s as a company that offered fraud-monitoring software for health-care claims. Carsanaro raised $5 million through two rounds of venture-capital financing in 1999 and 2000.[3]

As is typical with venture-capital deals, the investors received preferred shares with dividend rights. When the company ran into trouble, the founders were booted and the VCs took over. The VCs then oversaw seven more rounds of financing. In 2011, Bloodhound was sold for $82.5 million, but the original founders got a total of just $36,000. One cofounder apparently got a check for all of $99.

In their study "Renegotiation of Cash Flow Rights in the Sale of VC-Backed Firms," Brian Broughman and Jesse Fried explain that in more than half the venture-backed exits they studied, the founders got nothing.[4] Zero. And when the founders did get something from a sale, it was almost always a fraction of what their investors walked away with, thanks to the venture capitalists' use of convertible preferred stock. In fact, after studying 50 deals, they found only one case in which the founders got more than their venture backers. Remember, these are the start-ups that got venture funding. For every company a venture capitalist invests money in, hundreds get turned down.

I asked FreshBooks's McDerment why he hasn't taken venture capital despite having to bootstrap his first decade: "Outside capital is risk capital," said McDerment, "and it's a great opportunity to become misaligned. I would take a check [from a venture capitalist] anytime if we were truly aligned." McDerment was offered $25 million in venture-capital funding in November 2012 but turned it down because venture-capital funds need to eventually sell their winning bets in order to appease their investors.[5] McDerment didn't want to be forced to sell the company or take it public just because his investors needed liquidity.

The main benefit of outside money from a professional investor is that it is usually "smart money." Rather than your Uncle Arnie, who knows nothing about your industry, cutting you a check, venture-capital cash usually comes with some very smart people to help guide your business. Your newfound partners will be keen to see you grow and can provide connections and advice to help you expand. Venture-capital cash can also add jet fuel for the expansion of a winning business model. And when it is time to sell or raise another round of financing, your venture capitalist can also be instrumental in finding investors.

Cash Source 3: Charge Up Front

The third strategy is to flip the traditional subscription-business cash-flow model on its head so you're getting paid before you deliver the service. Instead of charging by the month, your company can charge for an entire year of your subscription up front.

In order to evaluate the impact of this strategy, I came up with a metric I call CUF:CAC, where CUF stands for *cash up front*, the amount of money your subscriber pays when he signs up for your subscription. CAC is your *customer acquisition cost*.

To see how your CUF:CAC ratio affects your cash flow, let's imagine two scenarios. In the first, following a typical subscription model, you charge $20 a month for access to your library of yoga instructional videos. Your cost to acquire a subscriber is $100, so your CUF:CAC ratio is 1:5. In other words, you're getting one dollar up front for every five you invest in winning subscribers. With this model, the more you grow, the faster you'll run out of cash.

Now let's imagine you change your model and offer your subscription for $199 a year, paid in advance. Assuming your cost to acquire a customer stays the same, at $100, your CUF:CAC ratio is now 2:1. With this strategy, the more you sell, the more cash you accumulate.

At TIGER 21, the elite investment club we looked at in chapter 5, members pay their $30,000 subscription fee up front each year. Similarly, at SellabilityScore.com, we offer subscribers a 16% discount if they pay for a year's worth of service up front. That means we get 16% less MRR from a customer who pays up front, but it also means our CUF:CAC ratio is positive on those sales.

Another way to improve CUF:CAC is to charge a setup or initiation fee. HubSpot cleverly disguises a setup fee (which no customer wants to pay) as a $2,000 Inbound Marketing Success Training package and charges it to new Pro or Enterprise customers to recover some of the costs of getting them set up. Without the $2,000 Inbound Marketing Success Training package, HubSpot would have a deeply negative CUF:CAC ratio.

Looking back at HubSpot's financials, in Q1 2012, the CAC was $6,880 and the MRR was $583. Assuming the company needed to pay all its sales and marketing costs in advance, its CUF:CAC ratio would have been a dismal .084:1. It would have received around $8.50 in the first month for every $100 it spent to win the customer. It would have taken HubSpot almost 12 months to recover the cash spent to acquire the customer.

By charging $2,000 up front for the Inbound Marketing Success Training package, the company's CUF:CAC ratio goes up to a more respectable .37:1, and it gets $37 in the first month for every $100 it spends to acquire the customer.

In HubSpot's case, the ratio is still negative, which means it needs the outside money of people like David Skok, but the owners can hang on to more of their equity because they need less money to fund growth. In order to grow your subscription business while minimizing the amount of cash you need from other sources, shoot for a CUF:CAC ratio north of 1:1.

To understand a company with an excellent CUF:CAC ratio, let's take a look at Cambridge, Massachusetts–based Forrester Research. Forrester's primary business is selling syndicated market research on a subscription basis to billion-dollar companies. By 2013 Forrester was generating roughly $300 million in revenue from 2,451 customers, including 38% of the Fortune 1000.[6]

Forrester's core product is called RoleView. For around $30,000 per year, chief information officers (CIOs) and chief marketing officers (CMOs) can get research insights delivered to them based on their functional role within their company. Each RoleView subscription typically includes access to research, membership in a Forrester leadership board where peers discuss issues they have in common, phone and e-mail access to the analysts who perform the research, unlimited participation in Forrester webinars, and access to one live event.

Forrester RoleView's annual subscriptions are mostly charged up front. The company gets an entire year's worth of its customer's money in advance, giving it a positive CUF:CAC ratio. George F. Colony, CEO and chairman of Forrester, noted the benefit of charging up front for subscriptions in his letter to shareholders in early 2013: "Forrester's business model yields healthy levels of free cash flow . . . we typically carry between $50 and $100 million in cash."

Blacksocks uses a similar cash-flow-positive model to grow its "sockscription" business. Instead of selling a $10 pair of socks, it sells a subscription: a customer pays for an entire year's worth of black socks—usually around $100—up front.

Charging up front for your subscription can lengthen the sales cycle and increase your cost to acquire a customer, but if you want to maintain control of your subscription business, it may be your best approach.

In summary, your LTV:CAC determines whether or not a guy like David Skok, or the thousands of other venture capitalists in the country, will want to invest in your business, while your CUF:CAC ratio will determine how much of an investor's money you'll need, and how much of your equity you will have to give up in the process.

CHAPTER 14

The Psychology of Selling
a Subscription

S o how on earth do you sell a subscription?

Selling a subscription is different than selling a stick of deodorant. With a subscription, you're proposing a relationship over time. Shifting from selling a one-shot product or service to selling a subscription is like the difference between a one-night stand and getting married.

In a subscription relationship, the customer agrees to stay loyal on a long-term basis, while you agree to keep your partner's interests at heart. Like all long-term relationships, each party is giving up a little bit of freedom in return for what he hopes will be a better deal in a committed relationship.

Customers may give up a little purchasing freedom when they subscribe, but there are a lot of benefits to subscribing rather than purchasing on a one-shot basis. A Zipcar subscriber, for example, can access an expensive car for a few dollars a month. A Mosquito Squad subscriber can invite his boss over for a barbecue on a warm summer evening, knowing the backyard is already protected from bugs. Netflix subscribers don't have to rent movies from iTunes at $5.99 each; they can pay less than $10 a month and have access to thousands of titles.

Subscription Fatigue

Increasingly, however, subscription businesses need to overcome the "subscription fatigue" that is deepening with every credit card statement we open.

There was a time when one or two ongoing charges showed up on our credit cards each month; it was easy to ignore the few dollars we spent on cable or car insurance. Today, we're buying a lot more on subscription, so those small monthly charges are adding up to a big nut each month. In addition, many of us have experienced the frustration of trying to turn off a sticky subscription or figuring out the origin of a credit card charge from an obscure subscription we bought years earlier. Increasingly, our bar for opting into a subscription relationship is getting higher.

Don Nicholas, CEO of the Mequoda Group publishing consultancy, has seen this heightened skepticism firsthand. "Increasingly we're hearing cautionary language around subscriptions in our customer focus groups," he says. "The consumer is aware that they are likely going to forget to unsubscribe."

So how do you convince a subscription-weary consumer to add yet another monthly charge to her credit-card bill? Every subscription business will be different, but here are seven ways to sell a subscription.

Subscription Selling Idea # 1: Think 10 x vs. 10%

Consumers are aware that a subscription relationship is much more valuable to you than a onetime purchase. So to get them to commit you'll need to give them a big return on their investment. A consumer with an acute case of subscription fatigue is unlikely to subscribe just to save 10%, but she might be convinced to subscribe if you could make a case that she will enjoy 10 *times* the value of the alternative.

For subscribers to the online art school New Masters Academy, $29 per month buys access to 350 hours of video tutorials. The going rate for a one-day in-person art class from a New Masters Academy instructor is $600–800, so you get access to 350 classes each month for around one-twentieth the cost of an in-person lesson. As New Masters Academy founder Joshua Jacobo said, "We provide a ridiculous amount of value."

At Genius Network, the private club subscription program for some of the world's leading entrepreneurs, Joe Polish promises prospects a 10x (10 times) return on their investment. Polish loans each new member an iPod preloaded with $80,000 worth of marketing "how to" content. The member can keep the iPod as long as she renews her subscription. Polish is so confident in his 10x promise that he tells new members that if they do not feel they are getting 10 times the return on their investment with Genius Network, he'd rather they not renew.

Netflix provides access to tens of thousands of titles for less than $10 a month. GameFly subscribers get 8,000 video games to choose from for a few bucks a month. Rdio provides a library of millions of songs each month in return for the cost of a fancy coffee. It makes economic sense to the customer to use these services instead of purchasing each DVD, video game, or song individually.

From 0 to 95,000 Subscribers in One Year

How much did you pay to print your last set of digital photos?

Every holiday season, we trudge down to the grocery store and print off some photos of our kids for our relatives who live in the UK. Last Christmas, I spent around $30 for a stack of happy snaps.

For exactly one tenth of the price, I could have subscribed to GrooveBook, a service that ships a bound book of 100 glossy 4x6 photos to your door each month. Each photo is perforated so you can remove your favorites and put them in a frame or on the fridge door. A hundred photos from the grocery store might cost you $30; if you use one of the online photo-printing companies, you could get the price down to around $20. But a GrooveBook subscription costs just $2.99 per month, and that includes shipping and handling. All you need to do is download the free application on your cell phone, upload 100 shots, and hit "submit." About two weeks later, you get a beautiful little book of your memories.

It's a 10 times better offer made possible because founders Brian and Julie Whiteman own their own printing press and have developed a patented technology that allows the book of photos to bend slightly when it is shipped, enabling them to mail a GrooveBook for 78 cents via the United States Postal Service.

By early 2014, after just one full year in business, GrooveBook was up to 95,000 subscribers—90% of whom are moms tired of the complexity and hassle of printing their photos at the grocery store. They are subscribing because GrooveBook is simpler and, at $2.99 per month, a 10 times better value than the alternative.

WhatsApp adds a million users a day because, at $1 a year, it offers at least 10 times the value of messaging through a mobile company that has customers paying north of $100 a year just to send texts.

Think "10 times" whenever there is an easy way for your customer to get your product or service without committing to a subscription.

Subscription Selling Idea # 2: Appeal to Their Rational Side

There was a time when people would subscribe just to say they had a subscription to something novel like razor blades or condoms. Those days are over.

The subscription business model has gone mainstream, and people are demanding that their subscriptions offer better value than the alternative. In short, we're buying more rationally.

Take Raz*War, for example. In March 2010, more than a year before Dollar Shave Club sold its first razor blade subscription, Raz*War, also a subscription razor company, won the People's Choice Award at Plugg, Europe's biggest start-up competition.

Within 48 hours of the Plugg announcement, 1,100 men—mostly technology geeks and early adopters—signed up for a razor blade subscription. At the time, early adopters were reading about Raz*War on TechCrunch and Springwise and wanted to be the first of their friends to say they had a subscription for razor blades.

Today, Raz*War subscribers behave much more rationally. They no longer see razor blades by subscription as a new concept they want to be the first to test, but they are still tired of going to the store to buy blades, only to find out the pharmacy is out of stock or the company has changed the blade handle again. Raz*War doesn't change the blade type (rendering old blades obsolete) as frequently as the competition, so customers feel they are just being sensible. They want a reliable source of good-quality blades without having to follow the constant upgrade dance of Gillette or Schick.

In our conversation, Raz*War founder Pierre De Nayer was quick to point out that being sensible is not the same thing as being cheap. Raz*War offers three types of blades, and 60% of De Nayer's subscribers opt for the most expensive model. Customers are still willing to pay more for high-quality razors, but they hate wasting money on a handle only to have it become obsolete when Gillette launches its latest product.

It's not just personal products that can be sold to individuals by appealing to convenience—it's hugely important when selling a B2B subscription. That's how H.Bloom built a business case for flower subscriptions. I spoke with H.Bloom's cofounder Sonu Panda in April 2014 and asked him how they sell a subscription to something as emotional as flowers. Panda told me that it starts with targeting a corporate buyer, like a restaurant owner or spa manager, for whom professional invoicing and reliability are important. Based on that knowledge, Panda coaches his sales reps to explain the H.Bloom approach to selling flowers, which sounds more like a logistics lecture than a Mother's Day sales pitch. They explain how flowers get from the farmer's field to a spa owner's countertop. Because of its volume and its subscription business model, H.Bloom offers hundreds of flower types, unlike the typical flower store, and bypasses the middlemen so customers receive their flowers within 48 hours of the farmer cutting them, as opposed to 10–14 days later for a smaller outlet. Further, H.Bloom does not require expensive retail space and can pass on some of those savings to the subscriber.

By the time the sales reps are finished, they have presented a fully rational case for why it makes sense to subscribe to a bouquet of flowers.

This strategy can work when selling a subscription to a consumer, but it is essential when you're selling a subscription to another business.

Subscription Selling Idea # 3:
Give Customers an Ultimatum

If given the choice, most consumers would prefer to keep their freedom and buy your product à la carte, on an as-needed basis. Depending on your appetite for building a subscription business, you may want to consider making subscriptions the only option for buying what you sell.

You can't buy a one-shot ticket to the Grano Speakers series; you can't pay $10 and download a single birth certificate from Ancestry .com; you can't walk into Staples and buy a box of Salesforce.com disks; you can't sign up for a one-shot TIGER 21 Portfolio Defense; and you can't buy a single movie from Netflix. These companies are 100% "all in" on the subscription model. They are giving their customers an ultimatum: subscribe or we can't do business.

The ultimatum strategy can be doubly important if you're targeting customers who are already buying from you on a one-shot basis.

I learned this one the hard way. When I first tried to remodel my research company from a sell/do service business into a subscription company, I wanted to have it both ways. We offered a subscription at the same time as we offered custom consulting.

We set up appointments with our best clients to introduce them to the subscription offering. A few bought, but most just listened politely and went back to doing business with us the old way. To them, it probably sounded as if the subscription business model was just another idea we were testing rather than an all-in bet on a new way of doing business.

After six months or so, we couldn't get enough customers to subscribe, so we had to turn off the subscription offer and go back to one-shot consulting.

A few years later, we made another run at switching to a subscription business, but this time we gave our customers an ultimatum: either subscribe or we can't do business. The difference in our customers' reactions was noticeable. They realized we were serious and took more time to understand the offering. They rightly assumed that if we were willing to bet our entire relationship on a new way of doing business, our offering must be worth it. In the end, most of our customers switched to the new model, and we never accepted another one-shot consulting client.

The main difference between my first failed attempt and our successful second move to a subscription model was our level of commitment. We forced customers to take the subscription or nothing.

Subscription Selling Idea # 4:
Give Them a "Freemium" Option

If you're going to force people to subscribe as your only pricing model, one way to overcome their anxiety about committing is to offer a free taste of what they will get from a full-blown subscription.

Mequoda Group's Don Nicholas found that it is virtually impossible to sell first-time visitors a subscription to an information product (e.g., a magazine or membership website) until they have first opted in to a free e-mail newsletter to sample the value of the content. Once they become an e-mail newsletter subscriber, they convert to a paid product at the rate of 3% to 30% per year, depending on the number of offers they are presented with and how carefully the publisher manages (e.g., weeds out undeliverable addresses and those who have opted out).

In this "freemium" model, you'll want to leave plenty of value *off* the table to instill a sense of intrigue about what the customer will get from subscribing. A good taster gives you just enough to assess the product but leaves plenty of temptations behind the curtain.

Use the freemium model when you have something that impresses your potential subscriber while still leaving them wanting more.

Subscription Selling Idea # 5:
Offer a Trial

If you have a product or service that is very hard to describe and that customers have to use before they will understand the benefits of subscribing, you may want to consider offering a trial. Unlike a freemium offer, which is typically available to a consumer forever, a trial usually has a start date and an end date.

Take a look at the trial subscription offered by Osler Bluff, a private ski club two hours north of greater Toronto; the area is home to roughly 6 million people, many of whom minimize the drudgery of a long, dark winter by downhill skiing on the weekends. Ontario, however, is not blessed with much in the way of vertical terrain, so the local ski spots are overrun with skiers. Arguably the best skiing can be found at Osler, but you can't just walk in off the street to buy a lift pass. Osler is a private ski club with a onetime $57,500 initiation fee, plus annual membership dues of a few thousand dollars.

That's a big nut to ski a small hill, but it's not just about the skiing. The après-ski is chockablock with investment bankers and law firm partners to network with. There is a playroom where the kids can be entertained while you get in some turns. Once the kids are old enough, there is a superb ski-racing program that has helped many youngsters develop into World Cup skiers. The main lodge is a beautiful post-and-beam clubhouse.

It's an entire experience, but selling it to customers requires that they see its value for themselves, which is why the company offers a onetime, $2,500 *trial* membership that buys a one-year glimpse into life at Osler Bluff, after which you're given the membership ultimatum: cough up your $57,500 or no more Osler for you. In any given year, between 90% and 100% of trial memberships convert to full memberships.

At FreshBooks, the cloud-based accounting tool used by more than 5 million people, when you click on the main navigation section, "Pricing & Sign Up," you don't see any pricing at all. Instead, you get a field prompting you to complete your company name and e-mail address as the start of your 30-day free-trial process.

I asked Mike McDerment, the cofounder and CEO of FreshBooks, why its pricing plans are not featured prominently on its pricing tab. While he would not reveal all of his trade secrets, he did say the company tests thousands of possible combinations of conversion funnels at FreshBooks, which leaves me to draw the conclusion that getting people signed up for a free trial is the *most important* first step in converting a user into a paid customer.

Zendesk, the customer support software that has grown from zero to more than 40,000 subscribers in seven years, also uses a free 30-day trial and invests all of its creativity in getting companies to use the product during the trial. I signed up for a Zendesk free trial to see how the company would try to move me from free user to paying customer. When I signed up, Zendesk offered me a series of five "getting started" videos, presented in a viewing pane with a checklist of "to dos." Each time I watched a video, I earned a check mark, and one less box was left unchecked. Like a child awarded a gold star for learning the alphabet, I was compelled to complete the five onboarding videos so none of the boxes would remain unchecked. Within a few hours of signing up, I got an e-mail from a real person who offered to help me get the most out of my trial. Later, the same person gave me a phone call to offer his help as I got started with Zendesk.

Throughout the free-trial process, Zendesk's focus was not on getting me to *buy* the product, it was on getting me to *use* it—a simple but important distinction. Zendesk knows that once you use its product, there's a greater chance of your becoming a subscriber.

Ancestry.com, which has tested thousands of conversion funnels over the years, currently uses an automatically converting 14-day free trial. When you sign up, you provide your credit card information and get instant access for free for 14 days. On the 15th day your card is charged. By asking for credit card information up front, the company is depressing its free-trial opt-in rate, but it has obviously done the math to know that getting card information first ultimately results in more paying customers down the road.

Conscious Box has tested thousands of trial permutations to acquire its 30,000 subscribers in under two years. CEO Patrick Kelly explained that the company's best-performing offer gives a prospect the first box for free. Conscious Box asks the trial subscriber to pay for shipping on the free box, so it collects credit card data on the subscriber. If the subscriber doesn't cancel after the first free box, the company starts charging the subscriber's card for each monthly box.

In some cases, the combination of a freemium version of a product *and* a free trial is the key to signing up a subscriber. At FreshBooks, for example, while the company offers a free 30-day trial of the software, a customer can also continue to use the free sample version, which is limited to billing just one customer. If you want to bill more than one customer, you need to start a paid subscription.

Free trials aren't limited to software. They work well when you have any product or service that is better experienced than described.

Subscription Selling Idea # 6: Offer Your Subscription as a Gift

Buying a gift is often a way to express how you feel about someone. If someone does you a favor, a thank-you gift expresses your appreciation. A birthday gift shows your love once a year. A wedding gift sends your best wishes.

The problem with a one-shot gift is that it's easily forgotten a few days after being received, which is why increasingly consumers are buying subscriptions for friends and family members as a way to express their appreciation over time.

Sock maker Foot Cardigan has about 2,000 subscribers to whom it sends a "delightfully unusual" pair of socks each month. Almost half of its subscriptions are bought as gifts.[1]

Standard Coca, a service offering craft chocolate on a subscription basis, estimates that up to 75% of its orders during a major holiday season like Christmas or Valentine's Day are gifts for other people.

BarkBox offers a one-, three-, or six-month subscription as a way to show your appreciation for the dog lover in your life.

A word of caution: the challenge is that gift subscriptions are notoriously difficult to renew. The consumer of the subscription did not make the original buying decision and therefore has to go through his own buying process in order to renew. The person who purchased the gift subscription is likely satisfied with purchasing a short-term subscription and is unlikely to pay for someone else to receive a subscription's benefits in perpetuity.

More than 400 people subscribe to Austin-based Nicely Noted, a curated surprise box of handcrafted stationery that subscribers receive each month. I spoke with Nicely Noted founder Perry Nelson, who talked about the challenges with gift subscriptions. For every 100 gift subscriptions, she estimates she will keep two or three as paying subscribers after their gift subscription runs out. By contrast, for every 100 regular subscribers who made their own decision to subscribe to Nicely Noted, she will retain more than 90 each year.

You can sell a gift subscription as a way to "top up" an already successful subscription offering, but given the lower renewal rates, avoid using it as your primary source of subscribers.

Subscription Selling Idea # 7: Set Fire to the Platform

From a consumer's point of view, the best part about a subscription offering is that it is always on. Unlike buying a concert ticket for a popular show that is sure to sell out, or a great sweater from a store that has only one left in stock, a subscription never goes away. The Netflix streaming service is always there; if you want to watch an old episode of *Top Gear* at three in the morning, all you need to do is log in. If you want to learn how to sculpt, you don't have to clamor for one of the eight workshop spots at the local art studio; you can simply fire up New Masters Academy when the impulse hits you.

This "always on" feature is fantastic for consumers but can be frustrating when you're trying to sell a subscription. If your service doesn't change from one day to the next, why should a prospect buy today? If the exact same offering is going to be available tomorrow, it is human nature to wait until you absolutely need to act unless there is something you will miss out on by procrastinating.

Therefore, as cheesy and clichéd as it is, one way to get people to subscribe is to set fire to the bridge and artificially simulate a burning platform that causes the customer to act to avoid losing something.

When our company subscribed to a marketing automation software provider, we spent a few months deliberating the decision. As we approached the end of the buying cycle, I was getting ready for a family trip. Sensing that the momentum of the sale was about to be lost, my salesperson put a compelling offer in front of us: sign up by the end of the month and the license would cost only $1,000 a month instead of the $2,400 a month the company normally charges. Saving almost 60% was a compelling enough incentive for me to prioritize the decision before I left for vacation. Did I think the same offer would have been available the next month? Yes, but there was enough of a doubt in my mind that it got me to act.

The burning platform strategy can, of course, backfire. If what you're offering is always on sale and you're always offering another deal, you train the customer to wait to see what offer will come next. Therefore, the very best salespeople set fire to the platform only when the customer has made the decision to subscribe and it is only a question of *when*. All it takes is a quiet, authentic conversation with your prospect who is already 95% of the way there. It's best not to publicize your burning platform offer; you want to avoid the perception that you are a discounter to people who are much earlier in the buying cycle.

You want customers to decide to subscribe to your offering on its merit alone. But, given that the subscription is always on, occasionally you may need to nudge their decision making and give them a reason not only to subscribe, but also to subscribe today.

This strategy usually works best when you have salespeople who can quietly and selectively communicate the offer to only those prospects who have decided to buy and are just dragging their feet on committing.

The Toughest Sale of All

So far we've been focused on selling subscriptions, but there is one preliminary sale you need to make before you sell your first subscription: you need to convince your employees and partners about the merits of the subscription model. Convincing your own staff to build a recurring revenue stream can be one of the hardest sales of all.

Andrew Gray, a partner at the Reading, UK–based accountancy Kirkpatrick & Hopes, was keen to move to the simplifier subscription business model for billing clients. Instead of billing by the hour, Gray wanted to switch his firm over to billing based on a fixed annual fee each year.

His idea was to sit down with his clients at the beginning of each year and estimate what it would cost to support them for the entire year. Once Gray and the client agreed on an annual fee, they would set up a monthly transfer to Kirkpatrick & Hopes from the client's account of one-twelfth the annual fee.

Gray's analysis revealed benefits for both his clients and his firm. Clients would enjoy the clarity and predictability of a fixed fee without feeling "nickel and dimed."

Gray reasoned that by switching to a subscription model, his accounting firm would also benefit from the steady flow of cash. In the old billing model, Kirkpatrick & Hopes would count hours in fifteen-minute increments and bill clients when the total reached £300. This meant that many clients carried a small balance with the firm. That was manageable on a single account but a significant cash drain across its entire customer base.

Gray knew both his customers and the firm would benefit from switching to a subscription model—but he didn't anticipate the resistance he got from his own employees and partners. They were hesitant to abandon the old way of billing clients by the hour, which was common in their industry.

Employee resistance to adopting a subscription model is common when you operate in an industry that has a traditional way of billing customers. Accountants, for example, have worked hard for the professional credentials bestowed on them by their industry's governing body. Therefore, if the industry has a normal way of billing customers, they are likely to stick to what is normal for the industry they have worked so hard to join.

Your first sale needs to be to your employees and partners, to explain the benefits they will enjoy from moving to a subscription model. The most compelling upside is that working for a subscription company generally makes employee workload much more predictable. Instead of having peaks and valleys of customer demand—daily, monthly, seasonally—you will have a predictable business and can staff for it accordingly.

Andrew Gray eventually won his partners and employees over to the merits of the subscription model. After getting them onboard, his next sale was to long-term clients who were used to paying for the firm's services by the hour. Gray explained to his existing clients that committing to a fixed monthly fee would mean they would always have Kirkpatrick & Hopes at their side. Gray's clients wouldn't need to hesitate to call the firm for a quick opinion on a financial matter. Gray also argued that by knowing their accounting fees in advance, clients could budget more accurately.

In the end, Gray was able to convince most of his clients to move to a subscription model. Today, 70% of Kirkpatrick & Hopes's monthly revenue of £75,000 comes from subscribers paying on average about £375 per month on subscription. Its annual churn rate is close to zero. Gray describes how moving to a subscription model has affected both his staff and his clients:

> **We and our clients have far greater clarity and control over their fee payments now: everything is agreed in advance. There are far fewer fee disputes and arguments that used to damage the working relationship with our clients. We also had a windfall of cash coming into the business equal to about 3 months' sales when we switched to the subscription model.**

In selling a subscription, you are asking a skeptical consumer to commit to a long-term relationship. If you do it right, they're locked in unless or until they decide to leave you. In the next chapter, we'll explore why customers quit subscriptions and what you can do to ensure that your customers stay loyal for as long as possible.

CHAPTER 15

Scaling Up

N ow that you have your subscription business running, it's time to consider scaling it up. I say "consider" because you may not want to become a giant business. Some owners, like Nev Lapwood, want to keep their companies purposely small.

Lapwood runs SnowboardAddiction.com, a membership website to which novice boarders can subscribe for tips and video tutorials on learning how to snowboard. He generates around $3,300 in MRR ($40,000 annually) from the site. The last time I spoke to Lapwood, he was taking a break from his life on the slopes of Whistler Mountain and using his subscription revenue to fund a mini-sabbatical on the beach in Thailand. There are probably plenty of lawyers earning 10 times what Lapwood makes who would trade places with him in an instant.

Similarly, at Nicely Noted, founder Perry Nelson has more than 400 subscribers paying $20 for her curated box of handcrafted stationery each month—and is OK with staying small. Her goal is *not* to be the next BirchBox but instead to create "a really healthy, comfy lifestyle business."

However, if you decide you want to expand and grow your subscription business, there are two main things you need to focus on. First, as we saw in chapter 12, you need to find a way to consistently acquire customers for no more than a third of their lifetime value. Second, you need to reduce the number of customers who cancel (churn).

Churn is often ignored in the early days of a subscription business because lost revenue from customers who leave is easily made up by new customers. But the larger your business becomes, the more corrosive effect churn has. Take a look at the math below

Example A: 4% churn at $10,000 MRR

Let's say you have $10,000 in MRR and a churn rate of 4% a month. That means you're losing $400 in MRR per month. If your product costs $100 per month, you have to go out and find four customers to replace the ones you lost. You can probably do that just from inbound inquirers to your website. Win five or more customers and you're growing your MRR.

Example B: 4% churn at $100,000 MRR

Now let's imagine you've got your business up to $100,000 per month in MRR but your churn is still at 4%. Now you're losing $4,000 per month in MRR and have to find 40 new customers to make up for the ones you lost. Even

though your churn rate is identical at 4%, you have to win 10 times the number of customers each month just to keep your revenue flat.

If we go back to the simple graphic Gordon Daugherty uses at Capital Factory, the higher your churn, the less LTV you capture:

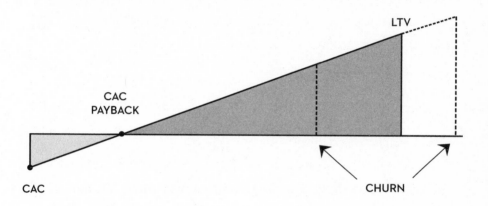

Some churn is unavoidable. In the case of Washington, DC–based Hassle Free Home Services, the number-one reason customers leave is because they move to another city. Its second most common reason for churn is that the customer dies.

A little bit of churn will always happen, and trying to winnow down your churn to zero is a futile battle. People move, couples divorce, some customers go bankrupt and others merge. There is a point of diminishing returns where eliminating all churn is so costly that you undermine your entire business model. It is the *avoidable* churn that leaves you running on a treadmill to nowhere.

The Treadmill to Nowhere

Most subscription businesses follow a traditional pattern of growth. Your MRR grows quickly at the start, and nobody pays much attention to churn. As each month goes by, more customers decide to leave, and replacing what you've lost each month becomes a bigger and bigger task. Then at some point you step on the Treadmill to Nowhere, where you can no longer acquire customers at the rate you're losing them. Your MRR starts to shrink.

The equation is simple:

New MRR = Churn Rate × MRR

As your MRR shrinks, you need fewer and fewer new customers to replace the ones who are leaving. At some point, your MRR drops to the point where you're able to replace the lost revenue with new customers you acquire in the month. You start growing your MRR again.

Then, like a boomerang, your growth stalls as your MRR builds to a point where you're losing more than you can replace again. Around and around in circles you go. The only way to start growing again is to get more efficient at winning customers or lowering your churn.

Lowering Churn

People may quit your subscription for any number of reasons related to the product or service itself. Your first step to reducing churn is to understand why people leave and to do what you can to improve your offering.

Beyond your product or service itself, there are some basic things any subscription business can do to lower churn.

Churn-Lowering Idea 1: Be a Rogue Jet

According to the International Air Transport Association, around 100,000 flights take off and land safely around the world every day.[1]

Have you ever wondered how all of those planes stay in the sky without hitting each other? Passenger aircraft fly on imaginary roads in the sky, with eastbound traffic flying at altitudes of odd numbers (e.g., 31,000 feet, 33,000 feet), whereas westbound traffic flies at altitudes of even numbers (e.g., 32,000 feet, 34,000 feet).

Two planes traveling toward each other in midair cross paths all the time, but one is flying 1,000 feet above the other. The pilots never have to react to an oncoming plane—unless, of course, a rogue jet gets onto the wrong flight path and disrupts their normal routine.

As you build your subscription business, your job is to be the rogue jet.

Somehow you need to disrupt the inertia that keeps your customers going about their daily routines on autopilot so you can insert your product or service and form a new routine for your customers. Churn is directly related to use: the more your subscribers use your service, the less likely they are to churn. The stickiest subscription businesses make it their mission to insert themselves into the daily lives of their customers. If your customers can avoid your product or service and still get their jobs done, you'll have much higher churn than if they need to interact with your service to complete their daily tasks.

Most men shave and use the bathroom daily, so most Dollar Shave

Club subscribers interact with a product provided by the company at least once a day. That's a much harder subscription to cancel than a magazine you read once a month.

At SellabilityScore.com, our sales reps use Salesforce.com, a subscription service that allows us to manage our customers' contact information and track our sales. We also use Salesforce.com as a calendar so our people know each other's schedules. Our salespeople track their daily goals in Salesforce so they know where they are every day based on their plan. We have since customized the platform so that we send quotes directly to our customers from Salesforce.

Salesforce is now fully integrated into our team's daily work flow—our flight path, if you will. We can't get much done in our company without logging into Salesforce. And because we've customized the platform and integrated it into our daily activities, the cost for us to switch to a competitive product like Infusionsoft would be high. As a result, we're a very sticky Salesforce.com customer.

As it turns out, we're not alone. Salesforce.com's monthly churn rate is around 1%. Even 1% is relatively high compared to companies like SAP, who are so integrated into the daily lives of their very large enterprise customers that they have annual attrition of around 5% and less than one half of one percent on a monthly basis.[2]

Churn-Lowering Idea 2: Watch the 90-Day Onboarding Clock

The air is crisp and you can feel the energy in the streets. As you turn the corner on the way into town, you notice a large monument lighting up the night sky and soon realize it is a clock. But this clock looks different. Instead of the numbers counting up, it's counting down. In

Pyeongchang, South Korea, this clock is counting down the days, hours, and minutes to the 2018 Olympic Winter Games.

Now imagine that the same clock is hanging above your office door. As soon as a new customer subscribes, the clock starts ticking down from 90 days. That's the time you have to successfully onboard that subscriber. Get it right, and she will continue to subscribe for years into the future. Botch the onboarding job and the likelihood she'll leave you increases and her expected lifetime value plummets.

Jason Cohen is the founder of four companies, including subscription-based WP Engine, a company that hosts WordPress websites. WP Engine onboards more than 1,000 new customers a month, and Jason thinks a lot about getting the first few months of a customer relationship right:

> **Consider the scale-ramifications of on-boarding 1,000 new customers a month. In that case, it's likely that any given server issue can affect a customer who has only been with us for 30–60 days. Thus the issue causes a "bad first impression," which is harder to address than a customer who has been with us for three years and therefore has built up a "bank account of patience."[3]**

Onboarding a New Banking Customer

You can think of a bank account as a subscription of sorts. You pay the bank a few dollars a month in return for account access through its online banking software.

For banks, the 90-day onboarding window is so critical that they have entire teams of managers who think only about how to get the first 90-day experience right with a new account holder.

Banking industry veteran Harland Clarke, a provider of integrated payment solutions, found that financial institution customers were most likely to close their accounts within the first three months of opening it. After the 90-day point, churn stabilizes as customers settle into the new account features. Harland Clarke also found that the window for a bank to cross-sell a new customer a second (or third) product is wide open in the first 30 days but shuts quickly after the first month.

Portrait Software, the UK-based subsidiary of Pitney Bowes, has also looked at the effects onboarding has on the lifetime value of a banking customer. As the company writes in a white paper:

> **By the time the clock has ticked for 90 days—the Customer Onboarding Period—the customer's lifetime value and profitability will have been practically set in stone.**
>
> **The first 90 days after any new account opening are an especially sensitive period characterized by several important customer experience factors:**
>
> - **Customers expect high levels of interaction.**
> - **They expect to be asked for personal information.**
> - **They are in "switch mode" and open to new offers.**
> - **They are much more likely to defect before "bedding in."[4]**

The importance of onboarding subscribers goes well beyond banking. At Nicely Noted, founder Perry Nelson writes a personal note to each of her new subscribers, signing off with a friendly "Keep in touch, Perry." Focusing on her onboarding experience has enabled

Nelson to keep her churn down to one or two of her 400 subscribers a month.

Don Nicholas, the publishing industry consultant with Mequoda, has seen the onboarding experience have a profound impact on the lifetime value of subscribers to magazines and subscription websites. Back in the early 2000s, Nicholas was the head of Blue Dolphin, a venture-backed company set up to sell magazine subscriptions online. Blue Dolphin would aggregate the content of a variety of publishers and distribute to a base of e-mail subscribers a selection of articles around a specific theme. Each article came with an offer for the reader to subscribe to the magazine that originally published the article.

One of the Blue Dolphin's products was a newsletter called *Women's Living*, which boasted 1.7 million subscribers. *Women's Living* aggregated content from 60 magazines, including popular titles like *Family Circle* and more esoteric publications like *Yoga Journal*. The editors of *Women's Living* started out spreading the content from the 60 magazines equally to ensure that all of them were covered in a balanced way.

Then the Blue Dolphin team decided to run an experiment, giving a cohort of customers articles from only the 10 best-converting magazines in the first 10 days of a *Women's Living* subscriber's relationship. To a traditional editor, the idea of blowing all your best content in the first 10 days was an anathema, but to a subscription marketer like Nicholas, it made sense.

One year later, when Nicholas and his team compared the lifetime value of the subscribers who had been given the very best content in the first 10 days of their subscription to the subscribers who had received a more balanced package of content from all 60 titles, the subscribers who received the "greatest hits" in the first 10 days were three times more valuable than the control group of customers. In other words, when Blue Dolphin packed a ton of value into the first 10 days of the relationship with a subscriber, it was able to *triple* the lifetime value of the average customer.

Fighting Inertia

One of the biggest reasons people stop subscribing to any service, whether a website like DanceStudioOwner.com or an investment club like TIGER 21, is the perception that they are paying for something they are not using.

Therefore, your biggest competitor for your subscription business is not the rival service; it is your customer's inertia in not using your service. For a subscription to stick, customers need to change their behavior and actually *use* the service. You have a short window to break your customers' old habits and insert yourself in their daily lives. That window is the first few weeks after they have purchased, before the excitement about what your subscription offers wears off.

When you sign up for a membership at LA Fitness, the company has a narrow window to get you to make the gym a regular habit. If it fails to get you into a new workout routine early, you'll give up your membership.

HubSpot reduced its monthly churn from 3.5% in 2011 to below 2% in 2013 and credits better onboarding as a big part of the reduction in churn. When I spoke to Frank Auger, vice president of services at HubSpot and one of the key architects of the onboarding experience, he outlined a four-step approach to onboarding: "First we do it manually to see what works," said Auger. "We then test a lot of things to try to optimize the onboarding experience. Once we know what works, we automate it. The last step is to integrate the learning into the software itself."

HubSpot used to focus on getting customers to attend 60-minute training webinars on major topics important to marketers. What it found through testing was that shorter videos, embedded directly in the software, worked better as onboarding exercises. "People don't want to sign up and sit through an hour-long webinar," said Auger. "When a new HubSpot customer wants to figure out how to accomplish a specific task, he would rather watch a three-minute video immediately."

At Hassle Free Home Services, company founder Jim Vagonis has designed an onboarding experience that includes an exhaustive inventory of a new home. When a new customer signs on, Vagonis dispatches a technician to complete an audit of the home, right down to the wattage of each lightbulb in a chandelier. That means that when something needs replacing, when the technician shows up for the monthly appointment, the replacement part is always in the van, and a second visit in the same month is rarely required.

The exhaustive audit up front also demonstrates to a new customer the depth of the service they have purchased and enables them to relax and let go of the management of their home. That's critical, because Vagonis has found that customers who completely delegate the management of their property are much more likely to renew their annual contract.

90-day Markers

Optimizing your onboarding experience is an inexact science that most subscription companies are always tweaking. The most challenging part of testing your subscription's impact is that you cannot immediately see the effect of your changes on your churn. You need to track a group of customers—most subscription companies call these "co-horts"—over time to see what effects your onboarding changes have on your customers' behavior.

Instead of waiting years to see if your changes are having the desired effect, you may want to consider 90-day markers. Doctors use high cholesterol as a marker for the likelihood that a patient will develop heart disease in the future. Likewise, you need a set of 90-day markers you can measure now that predicts an outcome (loyalty) in the future.

At SellabilityScore.com, we license our platform to our advisers (business coaches, accountants, etc.), who embed a piece of HTML code into their websites that allows them to offer our tools to their clients. If we can get new subscribers to successfully embed the code in their site and generate at least five reports in the first 90 days, they are much less likely to leave than if it takes more than 90 days to get them successfully using our tools.

Therefore, when we test onboarding tactics, we measure the effects the changes have on our 90-day markers. We have to wait for years to see the actual effect of an onboarding tactic on the lifetime value of a customer, but it takes only three months to see if the things we're trying have a positive effect on the markers we know are linked to loyalty.

Churn-Lowering Idea 3: Reduce Your Time to Wow

Learning to surf is hard. You've got to figure out how to get out to the break without being swallowed by a wave. Once you get there, you need to time the waves. Once you pick your favorite wave, you have to turn yourself around and start paddling with enough speed to match the pace of the swell. And once you're riding the wave on your belly, you need to figure out how to go from lying chest down on the board to standing—in an instant.

Any novice would quit the sport, if it weren't for little glimmers of hope. The moment you catch a wave for a second or two, you feel the rush of riding on a wall of water pushing you along, the feeling of your board carving into water as if it were a foot of fresh snow. Those moments on top of the wave can be blissful enough to give you the motivation to keep learning.

Like surfing, part of getting people to adopt your subscription product or service in the first 90 days is to give them a quick win that provides the motivation for them to learn more.

The e-mail marketing company Constant Contact started out using a "who, what, when" process for getting a new customer to start using its software. The first part of the process—logical for software engineers—asked users "who" they wanted to send their e-mails to. This forced new users to start with the tricky process of formatting and uploading an Excel spreadsheet of their contacts.

Constant Contact CEO Gail Goodman and her team realized that in order to upload a customer list, the users needed to leave Constant Contact and find their customer list somewhere on their hard drive or another service. The process of starting with the "who" was fraught with frustrations for the end user, who sometimes canceled the subscription to Constant Contact because of the complexity of uploading a customer list.

Goodman decided to shift gears and started the onboarding process with the "what." Instead of starting with spreadsheets, Constant Contact invited new customers to start designing their campaigns. Creating a campaign was the fun part that allowed customers to see their ideas come to life with pictures and templates. Only when the customer had invested the time in developing the "what" and been sufficiently wowed by how good her campaign could look did Constant Contact ask her to upload the list of contacts. This was a simple but important change that enabled Constant Contact to improve the first 90 days of a new customer relationship, and, ultimately, the average lifetime value of a subscriber. The difference was focusing on a quick and early wow for new subscribers. Goodman elaborates on Constant Contact's learning: "In the end, the way you work the funnel . . . is all about making sure that when someone tries or buys your product, they have a wow experience. They get quickly to an understanding and an outcome that blows them away."[5]

Churn-Lowering Idea 4: Charge Up Front

One of the secrets to driving more of the behavior change you need in the onboarding window is to charge up front.

Charging up front for your subscription means you're locking in a year's worth of renewals (unless you provide refunds) and getting your customer's cash up front. More important, it prompts a customer to make a bigger commitment to learning and adopting your subscription, making them much more likely to renew. When you cough up $5,000 for a subscription, you're a lot more committed to learning how to use it in the first 90 days than if you were paying $399 a month.

Wild Apricot is the software company I introduced you to in chapter 2 that offers companies an all-in-one way to manage their websites. It's a relatively complex solution with an e-mail platform, a fund-raising tool, and an event manager all built in. Wild Apricot's customers are typically managers of small not-for-profit organizations that have limited technical skills, making it critical that Dmitry Buterin and his team teach their subscribers how to use the platform once they have purchased it.

Buterin offers his customers a 10% price reduction if they prepay for a year. Fifty-two percent of his 7,000 customers pay in advance, and he has found that the bigger the up-front financial commitment a customer makes in the beginning, the more the customer commits to learning the tool. Charging up front has been one of a variety of strategies Wild Apricot has used to bring down its churn from as high as 8% per month to approximately 1%.

The cycle is intuitive: the more your customers pay up front, the more motivated they are to make the behavioral change needed to "get their money's worth." The more they adopt your service into their daily lives, the stickier they become down the road.

You may be wondering about the effect charging up front has on cancellations around the anniversary of the purchase. After all, a $2,000 charge on your credit card is a lot more noticeable than a $199 purchase. I posed that question to David Skok, the venture capitalist you met in chapter 12 and an adviser to many subscription businesses. "Charging up front actually reduces churn at the one-year point," said Skok. "The fact that you have charged up front means the customer invests more time to get to know your service, which makes them stickier in the long term." Most of the subscription company founders I interviewed for this book echoed Skok's findings. When customers pay up front, they make a deeper commitment to you and usually end up staying longer as a result.

Churn-Lowering Idea 5: Communicate like a Giddy Lover

Think back to the first real love of your life. My guess is you communicated a lot in the first few months of courting one another. There were daily phone calls, notes, and lots of face time. Then, as the excitement of your new bond was taken over by the comfort of a long-term relationship, the frequency of communications settled down into a steadier cadence.

Think of a new subscriber as a new lover. New lovers have a thirst to understand you intimately. An older subscriber will find your constant communication annoying after a while, whereas a new subscriber welcomes your contacts and takes the time to consume them.

After the 90-day mark, the new subscriber settles into the relationship, and overcommunication can actually cause churn. J. D. Power & Associates performed a comprehensive study of new retail bank customers and found that satisfaction peaked at five to six pieces of communication in the first year of service.[6] As you'll see from the chart below, satisfaction starts to drop with the seventh outreach.

2014 U.S. Retail Banking Satisfaction Study

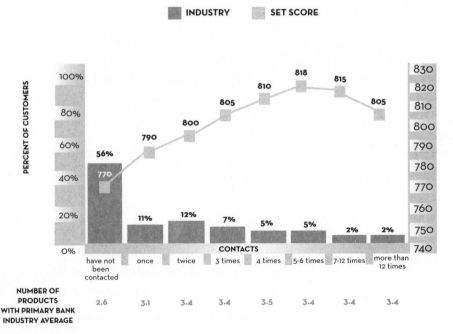

INDUSTRY   SET SCORE

While the J. D. Power & Associates study was specific to banking, the need to overcommunicate to new subscribers crosses all industries. Consider experimenting with various combinations of communication types, mediums, and frequencies to get the best results on your 90-day markers.

Churn-Lowering Idea 6: Drop a "Happiness Bomb"

As with any good relationship, it's important to keep a degree of spontaneity and surprise in your dealings with your subscribers. Lovers appreciate a small gift at an unexpected moment more than a big gift on their birthday. Often employees will appreciate a small but unexpected thank-you present more than a predictable annual bonus.

The best subscription companies always sprinkle in a little something surprising for their subscribers. BarkBox calls these spontaneous gifts "happiness bombs." Two of its 40 employees are dedicated to scouring its customer base for dogs who deserve a surprise. Each happiness bomb is sent with a handwritten note, which is no small feat considering BarkBox sent out 504 happiness bombs the month before I spoke to the folks there.

BarkBox's communications director, Chris O'Brien, tells a story of a subscriber who had lost one of her two dogs to old age. Both the dog parent and the remaining dog were heartbroken. When the BarkBox customer service team was alerted to the situation, it put together a special box of treats and toys for the dog who had lost its playmate.

Like BarkBox, Art Snacks leverages the surprise box subscription model and sends a curated box of art supplies to your door each month. Not only are the contents of the box a surprise; the company also includes a candy treat in each box that has nothing to do with the art supplies it is providing. The addition of a piece of candy is just a little something to surprise subscribers.

Even the granddaddy of all subscription businesses, Amazon Prime, may be experimenting with a happiness bomb–style strategy. In early 2014, the *Wall Street Journal* reported that Amazon had received a patent on "anticipatory shipping"; it uses your past shopping behavior to anticipate what you might like. In its patent application, Amazon reveals that "delivering the package to the given customer as a promotional gift may be used to build goodwill," suggesting Amazon may be planning to send Prime subscribers "happiness bombs" in the form of products they think customers will like based on their past buying behaviors.

As you build your subscription business, you will accumulate a truckload of data about your subscribers. Using that information to surprise them from time to time can go a long way to keeping the relationship alive and well.

Churn-Lowering Idea 7: Target Larger Businesses

If you target other businesses with your subscription service, your churn rate is going to be higher if you attract primarily small businesses. Therefore, one way to lower your churn is to target slightly larger businesses. Larger businesses are generally more stable. They have more employees and are less likely to change their business strategies on a dime.

By contrast, very small businesses and self-employed individuals often operate on the cusp of the job market. As the market becomes better, many self-employed individuals go back to working for someone else, causing churn for the businesses they deal with. Cloud-based accounting platform FreshBooks.com has more natural churn than Net Suite.com, another cloud-based accounting platform that targets larger businesses, because FreshBooks.com sells to self-employed people like dog walkers, graphic designers, and copywriters, who pop in and out of the job market as it expands and contracts.

Self-employed individuals are also much more price-sensitive because they don't separate their business and personal expenses as rigidly as larger companies. When money is tight on the home front, a self-employed individual will look for nonessential recurring expenses to chop. You could have the world's greatest subscription business, but if you're targeting very small businesses, you're going to have some unavoidable churn.

Note that you'll want to pick your target market in the context of your customer acquisition cost (CAC). While larger businesses tend to be stickier customers, they are also harder to win. Buying decisions have to be made by committee and involve multiple layers of approval. Purchases may need to be scrutinized by a procurement department, and purchase orders can take weeks to snail their way through the belly of a big company. Your CAC usually rises when you target larger businesses as a result of longer, more complex sales cycles.

Churn-Lowering Idea 8: Focus on "Net Churn"

Another way you can make up for lost revenue is to focus on upgrading your existing customers. Let's look again at Wild Apricot. In the fall of 2013, Wild Apricot had 6,400 customers paying them an average of $60 per month for an MRR of $384,000.

As you can see from the chart below, Buterin and his team have been working hard on lowering attrition over the past five years to the point where now they are at about 1% per month:

Attrition (aka churn) %

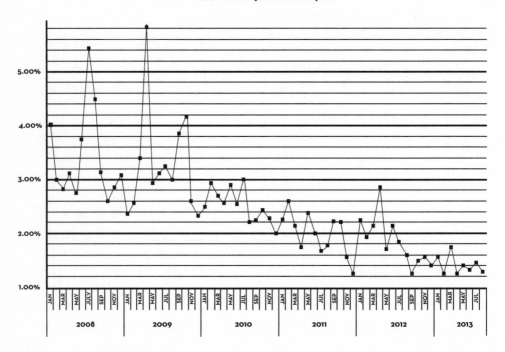

That means Wild Apricot loses around 1% of $384,000, or $3,840, in MRR per month. The good news is it also captures a lot of that lost revenue back from upgrading its existing customers. Wild Apricot pricing plans range from $25 to $200 per month. Its Community plan sells for $50 per month, while its Professional plan costs $100 per month. Therefore, if it's able to bump a Community subscriber up to Professional, it gets an extra $50 in MRR. If it upgrades 10 customers,

Wild Apricot has an extra $500 a month in MRR, and its net churn drops to $3,340 ($3840-$500).

Net Churn = Gross Churn–Upgrade Revenue

Your *net churn rate* is the calculation given above expressed as a percentage. Net churn of $3,340 as a percentage of an MRR of $384,000 is equal to 0.9% ($3,340 divided by $384,000 x 100).

Wild Apricot's net churn is approaching 0.5%, which means it is offsetting almost all of its lost revenue from churn with new revenue from upgrades. With its net churn close to 0.5%, it can grow quickly. Each new subscriber increases MRR, and today Wild Apricot has punched through the Treadmill to Nowhere and is now growing by 25% per year.

Churn-Lowering Idea 8: Reduce "Logo Churn" by Cross-Selling

Logo churn is the cardinal sin of any subscription company. It means that a company, or an individual in a business-to-consumer situation, has stopped doing business with you altogether. It means that you have to remove that company's logo from the list of happy customers on your website. Worse, you lose the permission to communicate with them regularly as a customer, which also means you'll have less opportunity to put a compelling offer in front of them and convince them to resubscribe.

Logo churn also means you break the regular billing cycle on a current credit card or your status as an "approved vendor" with an enterprise company's procurement department. It is a lot easier for a customer to switch on a new subscription when you already have a current billing relationship with them than it is to go through the hoops of setting up a commercial relationship for the first time.

The key to reducing logo churn is to offer a number of different subscriptions to the same company or person. If a customer decides one subscription is not right for them, allow them to turn off a single subscription while continuing as a subscriber to other services. You save the company as a customer, and you don't negatively affect your "logo churn."

Forrester Research offers its RoleView research subscriptions to various C-level executives within a big company. Procter & Gamble, for example, may subscribe to Forrester's RoleView for chief marketing officers and have a second subscription to a RoleView for chief information officers. If the CIO decides to cancel her subscription but the CMO keeps his, Forrester avoids any logo churn. It can tell Wall Street that P&G is still a customer, meaning the logo did not churn in the eyes of investors, even though one of the subscriptions was lost. More important than Wall Street optics, Forrester gets to continue a relationship with P&G and find a way to resell the CIO at some point in the future.

Dollar Shave Club started out selling a subscription to razor blades, but its goal has since evolved into "owning the bathroom." In June 2013, Dollar Shave Club launched its subscription for One Wipe Charlies—moistened cleansing towelettes for men. How can I say this delicately . . . it is selling a subscription to butt wipes. With a subscription to One Wipe Charlies, there is no longer a need to march down to the grocery store to buy the embarrassingly large 20-pack of dry, irritating toilet paper; Dollar Shave Club will send you a sleek pack of One Wipe Charlies in the mail. The company later also launched

Dr. Carver's Easy Shave Butter. Now it has three shots at keeping you as a customer even if you decide to turn off one of the subscriptions.

Churn-Lowering Idea 9: Go Evergreen

Magazine subscriptions have a start and end date. The problem with having an end date for your subscription is that it is extremely expensive and time-consuming to convince someone to resubscribe. At some mainstream magazines, the circulation department budget—the division of the magazine focused on acquiring and renewing subscribers—equals the total revenue the company gets from subscribers each year:

Total Revenue Per Year = Total Budget Per Year

If you have an end date for your subscription, attrition may not be because the product stinks; it could be that the subscriber changes her e-mail address or that he is on vacation when you send your renewal notice or is just having a bad day.

When the subscription-based razor blade company Raz*War first started, it offered a one-year subscription with an end date. Only about one in three customers renewed. The company was losing two thirds of its customers because it was asking them to proactively resubscribe. Today, Raz*War has gone to an evergreen model in which customers need to proactively turn off the service if they no longer want it. This has reduced its churn rate dramatically.

Marketers call an evergreen subscription a "negative option" because the customer has to exercise the option to cancel rather than being asked if she wants to continue. It may sound sneaky at first, but it is not intended to be. Assuming you're delivering a quality product or service, people don't want the hassle of telling you they want to keep resubscribing. It's like the needy lover who constantly needs reassurance about how much you care. Constant requests for validation get annoying after a while.

If it ain't broke, don't fix it. If you're Raz*War and your customer likes getting razor blades in his mailbox every month, don't make him fill out the forms associated with continuing the service—he'll let you know if he wants to stop. If you're Hassle Free Home Services and your customer likes having her burned-out lightbulbs changed each month, then keep up the good work and charge her card for the privilege. The "Set It and Forget It" value proposition loses its luster if you set it and keeping having to reset it.

The one exception to the evergreen rule is selling expensive subscriptions to large companies. Practically speaking, most large companies do not let their employees charge five-, six-, or seven-figure subscriptions on a credit card. In addition, most procurement departments want fixed-term contracts. From your perspective, most subscription businesses selling to large enterprise companies want the opportunity to renegotiate terms every year or two, so it generally works out better for subscriptions to have a fixed term and a corresponding renewal date.

In conclusion, the fastest way to scale your subscription business is to patch the hole in your bucket of customers. The first place to focus is the product or service itself—make sure it is something customers value. Then strive to get your voluntary churn as low as is practical by testing the nine ideas in this chapter.

CHAPTER 16

Reflections

As we've seen, the use of subscriptions is not just for media or software companies. With a variety of models to choose from, subscriptions can benefit any business in any industry. No matter the size, product, or service, subscribers are better for your business than customers. My favorite example of how a subscription company trumps a traditional one is the business of selling flowers.

Imagine for a moment the challenge of running a traditional flower store.

First, you have seasonality to contend with. The average flower shop generates almost half of its sales for an entire year leading up to just two occasions: Mother's Day and Valentine's Day.[1]

After major holidays, people buy flowers for birthdays and the odd dinner party, but in general, you're left trying to intercept some poor guy who has forgotten his wedding anniversary. If you're lucky, he buys flowers on his way home from work. If you're unlucky, he buys from your competitor down the street. Or worse, he forgets entirely and ends up taking his wife out for dinner—and your flower shop gets nothing.

To make matters harder, flower stores need to set up shop in a high-rent district. In a city like New York, London, or Hong Kong, you could easily spend more than $100 a square foot for pricey retail space.

Then there's your inventory. Flowers start to die the moment the farmer cuts them. Within three weeks, they are rotting in the retailer's fridge. It's not uncommon for a flower store to throw out half its inventory each month.

Perhaps there are some similarities in your business? Do you deal with seasonality? Lumpy demand? Are you constantly trying to intercept customers to make a sale? Do you have perishable inventory?

You may not sell something that dies, but if you employ people, one might make the case that you *do* have a form of perishable inventory. After all, employees work Monday through Friday and expect a paycheck whether you had the work to keep them busy or not.

I remember the frustration of trying to match the supply of people with demand in my consulting business. As consultants, we essentially rented people's time. If we guessed wrong and had too much work, our people became overwhelmed, morale suffered, our company culture deteriorated, the quality of our work plummeted, and our brand was tarnished.

If we had too little work, our people would hide behind their computer screens for fear of getting noticed. You could hear a pin drop in the office, and everyone worried when the layoffs would start. What's worse, all those people expected a paycheck, whether we had work or not, so our margins and profits would shrink for every day we guessed wrong.

Now, I've run two subscription businesses, and I can say definitively that I'd pick automatic customers any day of the week over the constant guessing game of trying to match supply with demand. Sonu Panda and Bryan Burkhart figured this out with their subscription-based flower company, H.Bloom. We traced its journey earlier in this book.

Companies like H.Bloom are the reason I wrote this book. H.Bloom took a traditional business, in an industry where subscriptions are not the norm, in a city thousands of miles from Silicon Valley, and decided to create automatic customers.

Mosquito Squad did the same thing in pest control, creating a subscription that takes one less thing off the average customer's "to do" list. Kathy and Suzanne Blake took their knowledge about running a successful dance studio and sold it on subscription, helping thousands of her industry peers build better businesses.

My hope in sharing these stories is that they will inspire you—no matter what industry you're in—to develop your own subscription business. I believe it will make your business less stressful and a whole lot more valuable. If I have sparked an idea for how you might create some automatic customers in your company, then this book will have served its purpose.

Acknowledgments

In the fall of 2013, I had just hatched the idea to write a book about recurring-revenue business models. My friend Actionable Books founder Chris Taylor recommended I meet with a soft-spoken Russian named Dmitry Buterin. Though Buterin and I had never met before, he took the time to patiently explain the subscription business model as he saw it in his company, Wild Apricot. With candor and humility, he detailed his journey to success in the subscription economy. Buterin lit the way for me to understand the intricacies of subscription models using his own company as a guinea pig.

One of Buterin's parting gifts was a list of other subscription-economy gurus whom he suggested I read up on, including David Skok and Jason Cohen. Thanks to both of them, as well as Jason's partner at Capital Factory, Gordon Daugherty, who helped me understand life-time value visually.

Don Nicholas, Anne Holland, and Tim Kerber educated me about subscribing to information online, while Amir Elaguizy explained the intricacies of an e-commerce subscription model. Joel York taught me about the math that underpins a subscription business, and Zane Tarence shared his hard-fought wisdom about how subscription-based software companies are bought and sold.

The list of subscription company founders and insiders who shared their stories with me is long. A few individuals stand out for their specific contributions: Frank Auger (HubSpot), Kathy Blake and Suzanne Blake Gerety (DanceStudioOwner.com), Anthony Centore (Thriveworks), Pierre De Nayer (Raz*War), Jason Fried (Basecamp), Andrew Gray (Kirkpatrick & Hopes), Verne Harnish (Gazelles), Sean Hunt (Stuart Hunt & Associates), Alex Hyssen (Køge), Joshua Jacobo (New Masters Academy), Jordana Kava (Standard Cocoa), Patrick Kelly (Conscious Box), Nev Lapwood (SnowboardAddiction.com), Kathy McCabe (Dream of Italy), Mike McDerment (FreshBooks.com), Perry Nelson (Nicely Noted), Mike Nevarr (Mosquito Squad of Northern Virginia), Chip Nyborg (Tri-State Elevator Co.), Chris O'Brien (BarkBox.com), Sonu Panda (H.Bloom), Joe Polish (Genius Network), Lori Rosen (Blacksocks), Jim Vagonis (Hassle Free Home Services), and Scott Zide (Mosquito Squad).

Friends Trevor Currie, Verne Harnish, Ted Matthews, and Dean Tai suffered through early drafts of this book and made it better with their input. Thanks to everyone who shared their stories.

A common approach among writers is to write to a person rather than a group. I can't remember who taught me that technique or where I heard it, but I found it helpful in writing this book. The person I write to is my sister Emma. She runs a successful company called DiG (Data Insight Group). DiG is a big success with blue-chip clients and smart people on staff, but Emma hasn't found her subscription model just yet. Every morning, I would sit down at my computer and try to peck out another 300-word letter to Emma that I never intended to send. After stringing together 150 mornings, I had my manuscript. You can imagine my anticipation when I actually shared a draft with her and asked for her feedback. When we met, her copy was littered with mark-ups. My heart sank, thinking she hated it. As it turned out, she did have lots of great suggestions, but she had also flagged a number of ideas to apply to her own business. Thank you, Emma, for being both an editor and my silent pen pal.

Finally, to my dad, who spent many nights around the kitchen table patiently explaining to me why subscribers are better than customers.

Recommended Resources

AutomaticCustomer.com

Visit AutomaticCustomer.com to download a variety of resources about building a subscription business, including a work sheet of the nine different subscription models and a description of whom they work best for.

SellabilityScore.com

Whether you want to sell your business next year or a decade from now, getting and improving your Sellability Score will allow you to rest easy, knowing you're building your business into a valuable asset. Companies that achieve a Sellability Score of 80 or above receive offers that are on average 71% higher than those tendered for a typical company. Complete the Sellability Score questionnaire and you'll get your score on the eight key drivers of sellability, including the Hierarchy of Recurring Revenue, which gives you a score on how well you've applied the ideas in this book to your company.

Built to Sell: Creating a Business that Can Thrive Without You by John Warrillow (Portfolio/Penguin)

In many ways, I should have written *The Automatic Customer* before my previous book, *Built to Sell*, since building recurring revenue is an essential first step to building a valuable, sellable business. Since you now understand how to build a subscription business, I recommend reading this book, which shows you how to run a company without letting it run you.

ForEntrepreneurs.com

David Skok's blog is a great resource for subscription-based software companies that are keen on attracting venture capital.

ASmartBear.com

Jason Cohen is a business owner and investor who writes a blog with a focus on cloud-based software companies.

Chaotic-Flow.com

Joel York blogs about the math behind building a successful subscription business.

Cratejoy.com

Amir Elaguizy's software platform is custom built for subscription-based e-commerce companies that ship a physical product.

Notes

CHAPTER 1: WHO WINS IN THE SUBSCRIPTON ECONOMY?

1. Stone, Brad, "What's in Amazon's Box? Instant Gratification," *Bloomberg Businessweek*, November 24, 2010. businessweek.com/magazine/content/10_49/b4206039292096.htm.

2. Tuttle, Brad, "Amazon Prime: Bigger, More Powerful, More Profitable than Anyone Imagined," *Time*, March 8, 2013. business.time.com/2013/03/18/amazon-prime-bigger-more-powerful-more-profitable-than-anyone-imagined.

3. Stone, "What's in Amazon's Box? Instant Gratification."

4. Bensinger, Greg, "Amazon Expands Grocery Business," *Wall Street Journal*, June 5, 2013. online.wsj.com/news/articles/SB1000142412788732479890457852 6820771744676.

5. Bishop, Jeff. "Bezos: Amazon Closer to Solving Economics of Grocery Delivery," *GeekWire*, May 24, 2013. geekwire.com/2013/jeff-bezos-amazon-fresh-closer-solving-economics-grocery-delivery.

6. Perez, Sarah, "Target Launches Its First Subscription-Based E-Commerce Service, Focus for Now Is Baby-Care Items," *Techcrunch*, September 25, 2013. techcrunch.com/2013/09/25/targets-launches-its-first-subscription-based-e-commerce-service-focus-for-now-is-baby-care-items.

7. Weber, Johannes, "Strassburg, 1605: The Origins of the Newspaper in Europe," *German History*, July 2006, 387–412. gh.oxfordjournals.org/content/24/3/387.abstract.

8.   "The Media's Risky Paywall Experiment: A Timeline," *The Week*, July 30, 2010. theweek.com/article/index/205465/the-medias-risky-paywall -experiment-a-timeline.

9.   Baker, Annie, "The New York Times Company (NYT) Hits 700,000 Paid Digital Subscribers," *Pulse 2.0*, May 20, 2013. pulse2.com/2013/05/20/the-new-york -times-company-nyt-hits-700000-paid-digital-subscribers-86287.

10. Gopal, Prashant, and Clea Benson, "American Dream Slipping as Homeown- ership at 18-Year Low," *Bloomberg News*, July 30, 2013. bloomberg.com/news /2013-07-30/american-dream-erased-as-homeownership-at-18-year-low.html.

11. Swartz, Angela, "BarkBox's Matt Meeker Has Big Plans for Pet Projects (Q& A)," *AllThingsD*, July 3, 2013. allthingsd.com/20130703/barkboxs-matt-meeker -has-big-plans-for-pet-projects-qa/.

12. Savitz, Eric, "The End of ERP," *Forbes*, February 9, 2012. forbes.com/sites /ciocentral/2012/02/09/the-end-of-erp.

CHAPTER 2: WHY YOU NEED AUTOMATIC CUSTOMERS

1.   Erickson, Heather, "Ancestry.com LLC Reports Fourth Quarter and Full Year 2012 Financial Results," Ancestry.com, press release, March 28, 2013. ir.ancestry.com/releasedetail.cfm?ReleaseID=752199.

2.   Bruder, Jessica, "Starting the 'Netflix of Flowers,'" *New York Times*, Septem- ber 22, 2011. boss.blogs.nytimes.com/2011/09/22/trying-to-start-the-netflix -of-flowers.

3.   Ibid.

4.   Smith, Jacquelyn, "Birchbox Cofounders Win Leadership Award at Forbes Women's Summit," *Forbes*, May 9, 2013. forbes.com/sites/jacquelynsmith /2013/05/09/birchbox-cofounders-win-leadership-award-at-forbes-womens -summit.

5.   Casserly, Meghan, "Birchbox Proves Try and Buy: Half of All Subscribers Make Full-Size Purchases," *Forbes*, August 15, 2013. forbes.com/sites /meghancasserly/2013/08/15/birchbox-proves-try-and-buy-half-of-all -subscribers-make-full-size-purchases.

CHAPTER 3: THE MEMBERSHIP WEBSITE MODEL

1. Doctorow, Cory, "Saying Information Wants to Be Free Does More Harm than Good," *Guardian*, May 18, 2010. the guardian.com/technology/2010/may/18/information-wants-to-be-free.

2. "Revolution Dancewear Acquires Top Industry Online Resource Center DanceStudioOwner.com," press release, June 5, 2013, Revolution Dancewear.com. revolutiondance.com/revolution-dancewear-acquires-top-industry-online-resource-center-dancestudioowner-com-pages-186.php.

CHAPTER 4: THE ALL-YOU-CAN-EAT LIBRARY MODEL

1. "Apple Launches the iTunes Music Store," Apple, press release, April 28, 2003. apple.com/pr/library/2003/04/28Apple-Launches-the-iTunes-Music-Store.html.

2. Fixmer, Andy, "Apple's 10-Year-Old iTunes Loses Ground to Streaming," *Bloomberg Businessweek*, April 25, 2013. businessweek.com/articles/2013-04-25/apples-10-year-old-itunes-loses-ground-to-streaming.

3. "Ancestry.com Unveiled More than 90 Million U.S. War Records," *New York Times*, May 24, 2007. nytimes.com/2007/05/24/technology/24iht-lineage.1.5851172.html.

4. Ibid.

CHAPTER 5: THE PRIVATE CLUB MODEL

1. Russell, Mark, "Private Clubs Cut Fees as Golfers Find Less Time for Tee," *Sunday Age*, January 17, 2010. newsstore.fairfax.com.au/apps/viewDocument.ac;jsessionid=EDEC72100CFB2E466A2A2353EE4EE47Fsy=afr&pb=all_ffx&dt=selectRange&dr=1month&so=relevance&sf=text&sf=headline&rc=10&rm=200&sp=brs&cls=19059&clsPage=1&docID=SAG100117MG3BA5GE1R9.

2. Sullivan, Paul, "Financial Advice Gleaned from a Day in the Hot Seat," *New York Times*, June 17, 2011. nytimes.com/2011/06/18/your-money/asset-allocation/18wealth.html.

CHAPTER 6: THE FRONT-OF-THE LINE MODEL

1. "Premier Success Plans," Salesforce.com, last modified March 12, 2014. www2.sfdcstatic.com/assets/pdf/datasheets/DS_SuccessPlans.pdf.

2.   "Mission Critical Success," Salesforce.com, last modified July 7, 2013. www2
      .sfdcstatic.com/assets/pdf/datasheets/MCS_Datasheet.pdf.

CHAPTER 7: THE CONSUMABLES MODEL

1.   Dahl, Darren, "Riding the Momentum Created by a Cheeky Video," *New York
      Times*, April 10, 2013. nytimes.com/2013/04/11/business/smallbusiness
      /dollar-shave-club-from-viral-video-to-real-business.html.

2.   Bryant, Martin, "Dollar Shave Club's CEO on Life after THAT Video and What
      the Company Did Next," *The Next Web*, November 6, 2013. thenextweb.com
      /video/2013/11/06/dollar-shave-clubs-ceo-life-video-company-next.

3.   "Logistics News: Amazon to Add 18 New Distribution Centers Worldwide in
      2012 as It Keeps Investing in Logistics," *Supply Chain Digest,* August 7, 2012.
      scdigest.com/ONTARGET/12-08-07-1.php.

4.   Urstadt, Bryant, "What Amazon Fears Most: Diapers," *Bloomberg Business-
      week*, October 7, 2010. businessweek.com/magazine/content/10_42
      /b4199062749187.htm.

5.   "Amazon.com to Acquire Diapers.com and Soap.com," Amazon.com, press
      release, November 7, 2010. phx.corporate-ir.net/phoenix.zhtml?c=176060&p
      =irol-newsArticle&ID=1493202.

6.   Del Rey, Jason, "Dollar Shave Club Lands $12 Million Investment to Dramati-
      cally Expand Product Portfolio," *All Things D*, October 8, 2013. allthingsd
      .com/20131008/dollar-shave-club-nabs-12-million-to-dramatically-expand
      -product-portfolio-and-create-lifestyle-content.

7.   Popken, Ben, "Does Dollar Shave Really Save?" *MarketWatch*, April 20, 2012.
      marketwatch.com/story/does-dollar-shave-really-save-1334930885394.

CHAPTER 8: THE SURPRISE BOX MODEL

1.   "Pet Humanization: Products Traditionally Reserved for Humans Are Expand-
      ing into the Animal World," TrendHunter.com, trendhunter.com/protrends
      /pet-humanization-products-traditionally-reserved-for-humans-are
      -expanding-i.

2.   Meeker, Matt, "Like to Spoil your Dog? BarkBox May Be for You," video,
      Bloomberg TV, November 14, 2013. bloomberg.com/video/like-to-spoil-your
      -dog-barkbox-may-be-for-you-AyS_LhZFQ7~iIL_e~cTi7w.html.

3. "What Kind of Items Are Included in a BarkBox?" Barkbox.com, June 10, 2014. faq.barkbox.com/customer/portal/articles/912347-what-kind-of-items-are -included-in-a-barkbox-.

4. "Where Are Items Made? Are They Safe for My Pup?" Barkbox.com, February 17, 2014. faq.barkbox.com/customer/portal/articles/927966-where-are -items-made-are-they-safe-for-my-pup.

CHAPTER 9: THE SIMPLIFIER MODEL

1. Schilling, Mary Kaye, "Secrets of the Most Productive People," *Fast Company*, November 18, 2013. fastcompany.com/3021377/pharrell-get-busy.

2. Williamson, Elizabeth, "What Sequester? Washington Booms as a New Gilded Age Takes Root," *Wall Street Journal*, May 31, 2013. online.wsj.com/news /articles/SB10001424127887323798104578455311507007562.

3. Ewing, Samara Martin, "Norton Manor: Frank Islam and Debbie Driesman's Pride of Potomac," WUSA9, November 28, 2013. wusa9.com/news/local /story.aspx?storyid=284279.

CHAPTER 10: THE NETWORK MODEL

1. Smith, Laura, "First Commercial Telephone Exchange—Today in History," ConnecticutHistory.org. connecticuthistory.org/the-first-commercial -telephone-exchange-today-in-history.

2. Goetz, Jim, "Four Numbers That Explain Why Facebook Acquired WhatsApp," *Sequoia*. sequoiacapital.tumblr.com/post/77211282835/four-numbers-that -explain-why-facebook-acquired.

3. Hart, Myra M., Michael J. Roberts, and Julia D. Stevens, "Zipcar: Refining the Business Model," Harvard Business School, May 9, 2005. newentrepreneur ship.files.wordpress.com/2012/01/zipcar-refining-the-business-model.pdf.

4. Clifford, Stephanie, "How Fast Can This Thing Go, Anyway?" *Inc.*, March 1, 2008. inc.com/magazine/20080301/how-fast-can-this-thing-go-anyway.html.

5. Ibid.

6. Naughton, Keith, "Avis Budget Embraces Car Sharing with Zipcar Acquisition," Bloomberg News, January 2, 2013. bloomberg.com/news/2013-01-02/avis -budget-makes-491-million-offer-to-acquire-zipcar.html.

7. "Number of World of Warcraft Subscribers from 1st Quarter 2005 to 3rd
    Quarter 2014 (in millions)," Statista. statista.com/statistics/276601
    /number-of-world-of-warcraft-subscribers-by-quarter.

8. Patrick, Brian, "Zipcar Timeline: From Business Idea to IPO to $500 Million Buy-
    out," *Entrepreneur*, January 2013. entrepreneur.com/blog/225399.

9. WhatsApp company overview, CrunchBase. crunchbase.com/company
    /whatsapp.

CHAPTER 11: THE PEACE-OF-MIND MODEL

1. Freeman, Mike, "Qualcomm Sells Stake in Tagg—The Pet Tracker," *UT San
    Diego*, July 10, 2013. utsandiego.com/news/2013/Jul/10/Qualcomm-Tagg-Pet
    -Tracker-Private-Equity.

2. "Salesforce.com Signs Definitive Agreement to Acquire Radian6, the Industry's
    Leading Social Media Monitoring Platform," Salesforce.com, press release,
    March 30, 2011. salesforce.com/ca/company/news-press/press-releases/2011
    /03/110330.jsp.

3. "Berkshire's Corporate Performance vs. the S&P 500," Berkshire Hathaway,
    February 26, 2010. berkshirehathaway.com/letters/2009ltr.pdf.

CHAPTER 12: THE NEW MATH

1. Colao, J. J., "In Defense of the Lifetime Value (LTV) Formula," *Forbes*, Septem-
    ber 13, 2012. forbes.com/sites/jjcolao/2012/09/13/a-dangerous-seduction
    -revisited-in-defense-of-the-lifetime-value-ltv-formula. All values based on this
    source.

2. "Ancestry.com Inc. Reports Q2 2012 Financial Results," Ancestry.com, press
    release, July 25, 2012. ir.ancestry.com/releasedetail.cfm?ReleaseID=695393.

3. Nunogawa, Matt, "Notes and Summary of Gail Goodman's 'The Long Slow
    SaaS Ramp of Death,'" @amattn, September 11, 2013. amattn.com/p/notes
    _summary_long_slow_saas_ramp_of_death.html.

CHAPTER 13: THE CASH SUCK VS. THE CASH SPIGOT

1. Botteri, Philippe, et al., "Bessemer's Top 10 Laws of Cloud Computing and
    SaaS," Bessemer Venture Partners, Winter 2010. bvp.com/sites/default/files
    /bvps_10_laws_of_cloud_saas_winter_2010_release.pdf.

2. McDerment, Mike, "An Open Letter from FreshBooks Founder Mike McDerment," FreshBooks.com, August 21, 2012. freshbooks.com/cloud-accounting -Letter.

3. Davidoff, Steven M., "In Venture Capital Deals, Not Every Founder Will Be a Zuckerberg," *New York Times*, April 30, 2013. dealbook.nytimes .com/2013/04/30/in-venture-capital-deals-not-every-Founder-will-be-a -Zuckerberg.

4. Broughman, Brian, and Jesse Fried, "Renegotiation of Cash Flow Rights in the Sale of VC-Backed Firms," *Journal of Financial Economics*, March 2010, 384–99. leeds-faculty.colorado.edu/bhagat/RenegotiationCashFlow RightsVC.pdf.

5. Levy, Ari, "No VC: FreshBooks CEO Sees Risk Capital as Too Risky," Bloomberg News, November 26, 2012. go.bloomberg.com/tech-deals/2012-11-26-no-vc -freshbooks-ceo-sees-risk-capital-as-too-risky.

6. "Corporate Fact Sheet," Forrester Research, last modified December 31, 2013. forrester.com/staticassets/marketing/about/Fact_Sheet.pdf.

CHAPTER 14: THE PSYCHOLOGY OF SELLING A SUBSCRIPTION

1. Newman, Andrew Adam, "Sock-of-the-Month Clubs Rise Online, Bringing Subscriptions to Feet," *New York Times*, December 3, 2013. nytimes.com/2013 /12/04/business/media/sock-of-the-month-clubs-rise-online-bringing -subscriptions-to-feet.html.

CHAPTER 15: SCALING UP

1. Pollak, Sorcha, "2012 Was the Safest Year Ever to Travel by Plane," *Time*, February 28, 2013. newsfeed.time.com/2013/02/28/2012-was-the-safest-year -ever-to-travel-by-plane.

2. "What Does Salesforce.com Have in Common with High-Margin Software Businesses? Not Much," Seeking Alpha, October 2, 2013. seekingalpha.com /article/1726272-what-does-salesforce-com-have-in-common-with-high -margin-software-businesses-not-much.

3. Cohen, Jason, "LARGE x RARE == DIFFERENT: Why Scaling Companies Is Harder than It Looks," A Smart Bear, January 28, 2014. blog.asmartbear.com /scaling-startups.html.

4.   "Customer Onboarding in Retail Financial Services," Pithey Bowes, portrait
      software.com/resources/white-papers/customer-onboarding-retail-financial
      -services.

5.   Nunogawa, Matt, "Notes and Summary of Gail Goodman's 'The Long, Slow
      SaaS Ramp of Death,'" @amattn, September 11, 2013. amattn.com/p/notes
      _summary_long_slow_saas_ramp_of_death.html.

6.   "10 Strategies for an Award-Winning Onboarding Process," Harland Clarke,
      last modified July 25, 2012. harlandclarke.com/files/user/page316
      /10_Strategies_for_Onboarding-071712.pdf.

CHAPTER 16: REFLECTIONS

1.   "Florists" Industry Reports," HighBeam Research, accessed October 8, 2014,
      business.highbeam.com/industry-reports/retail/florists.

Index